One Word at a Time:

Finding Your Way as an Indie Author

Eric Vance Walton

This book is copyright 2014 Eric Vance Walton. All Rights Reserved. Do no duplicate, distribute, or reproduce without explicit permission from Eric Vance Walton or Authors Publish Press.

Authors Publish Press
Bow, Wa

Contact: support@authorspublish.com
www.AuthorsPublish.com/Press/

ISBN: 978-1-942344-00-1

Table of Contents

Introduction xi

PART I:
The Writing Life 1

Chapter One:
The Life of a Writer with a Full Time Job 3

Chapter Two:
What I Learned From Writing My First Novel 13

Chapter Three:
What is Your Definition of a Successful Writing Career? 21

Chapter Four:
Is Self-Publishing A Good Fit For You? 27

Chapter Five:
Achieving Work-Life Balance By Finding Your
Ideal Writing Ritual 37

Chapter Six:
Things That Will Bring You Back To The Writing Zone 45

Chapter Seven:
Ways To Stay Motivated To Write 53

Chapter Eight:
Cast Aside Your Fears and Say Yes To Success........................ 61

Chapter Nine:
Balancing The Books 67

Chapter Ten:
What I Wish I knew As A Beginning Writer............................. 79

PART II:
On Writing.. 85

Chapter Eleven:
Crafting the First Draft of Your Novel... 87

Chapter Twelve:
Tips on Writing (and Completing) Your Debut Novel 109

Chapter Thirteen:
Overcoming Writer's Block...117

Chapter Fourteen:
Editing and Revising your Novel 123

PART III:
Marketing Your Book..147

Chapter Fifteen
Applying Lessons Learned in the Business World..............149

Chapter Sixteen
Studying Success 155

Chapter Seventeen:
Adopting the Collaborative Mentality 161

Chapter Eighteen:
Ways to Build Your Audience Online 167

Chapter Nineteen:
Ways to Build Your Audience Offline 175

Chapter Twenty:
The Potential Role of Literary Journals 185

Additional Resources 193

Indie: a short form of "independence" or "independent".

Indie Author: a writer who publishes outside of the mainstream publishing industry.

Indie Book: An indie book is any book that is published through a small press or self published by the author.

Introduction

There is a revolution happening right now. If you're a writer, you are part of it, even if you don't realize it. Technology has provided authors with all of the tools needed to become successful. The success that once depended on being accepted by a major publisher is now within your grasp. Today, the only thing standing between you and living your ideal writer's life is figuring out how to use all of these powerful tools to your advantage. This isn't easy but it is attainable.

What does living the writer's life mean to you? Living the writer's life to me simply means taking this incredible gift of words and honoring it by allowing writing to play the role in your life it deserves. The size of this role is different for everyone and will fluctuate as your writing career progresses. One thing is universal: with all of the demands placed on us, even making room for writing in your life takes work. To truly become a successful Indie author you must make up your mind that, finally, you will prove to the world and to yourself how important this gift of words is to you. After all, writing isn't just something we do, it is something we are.

There are countless books on the market about the mechanics of writing but many people in the world can write well. After a few decades in the writing business, I noticed that writers really need a resource to show them how to achieve their dreams using their craft. After all, I had struggled with this for years myself, so I decided that I needed to write a book about how to effectively live a successful writer's life. I have a lot of wishes for this book but more than anything I hope to save you from making the same mistakes that I did. With this book I hope to provide you the gift of a shortcut to success and the ability to achieve the elusive writer's life.

Is it your ultimate dream to become a professional writer but you're not sure where to begin? Do you feel stuck and don't know how to take your writing career to the next level? Would you like to learn easy and effective ways to use social media to its fullest potential? If the answers to any of these questions are yes, then shake off your apprehensions, open your mind, and read on.

I've been writing for the better part of the last two decades while working a full time job. I'm the first to admit that I have made almost every mistake a writer could make. Along the way I have learned to embrace failure as a lesson and, with each misstep I have readjusted my approach. As I became more familiar with the writing community, a couple things became apparent. I noticed that very few people can successfully juggle the demands of life, a day job, and achieving success as a professional writer.

What I've learned is with dedication, humility, and persistence, finding success as an Indie writer is easier now than it has ever been. Technology has given the Indie writer a tremendous amount of power and many more options in achieving their goals; the trick is to learn how to use all of these amazing tools to your advantage. Nothing is more thrilling to me than putting food on the table or purchasing something for my family with the proceeds earned from my written words.

My first toddling steps toward building a writing career began in the early nineties. In my heart I knew that I was born to write but had no clue how to make a living with it. Over the following decade and a half, I wrote poetry, editorials, did freelance magazine work, created a comic strip for a regional newspaper, entered contests, and self-published five books in various genres while working a full time job. In hindsight, I realize I approached my writing career in a very unfocused way. Still, in the back of my mind,

I always felt as though my big break was just around the next bend.

The turning point for me was the day I turned forty years old. The feeling that I would make a career of writing began to fade as I reflected on how hard I had worked on my writing over the last sixteen years and how little I had to show for it. People who were once my peers at work had long ago left me far behind on the corporate ladder because I was focusing so much of my energy on my writing career. It was during this period of reflection I decided to give myself the gift of just one more year, twelve months to complete my coup de grace, my first novel. If it didn't go well, I was going to have to be realistic, admit defeat and focus on advancing in my regular career. But the thought of not waking up in the morning excited about the next writing project gave me an ache in the pit of my stomach.

I dusted off a novel I had started eight years

earlier but never had the guts to finish and threw all of my being into it. I wrote as if my life depended upon it because I realized in many ways, it did. I knew that to stop writing would mean to stifle a very special part of my soul. I took out a loan and hired a professional to edit my first draft, I did the rewrite and after almost a year to the day, my first novel was completed. That year of writing and editing was like boot camp for me. I learned more than I ever thought I could.

I self-published that first novel, "Alarm Clock Dawn," and this is precisely when the magic began to happen. All of a sudden, wonderful people began to appear in my life just when I needed them. These people offered me guidance or helped to open a door that was previously closed to me. My writing career began to grow in quantum leaps and before I knew it, I had readers from all over the world! It was almost as though I had to set all of my doubt and fears aside and finally prove to the Universe how serious I was about being a writer before everything fell into place.

From that day on, each new step up the ladder of my writing career wasn't scary at all, it felt exhilarating and as natural as breathing. I felt a rush of intense creativity, freedom, and contentment like I never experienced before. After finally experiencing first-hand how wonderful it is to live the writer's life, I decided that I needed to share this gift with others. This is precisely how the idea for this book came into being.

If you take nothing else away from this book, please understand that achieving the writer's life is worth every effort it takes to achieve it. I promise you two things, this journey will be both more difficult and more rewarding than you can even imagine.

The great reward at the end of all of this difficult work will be a heart absolutely overflowing with contentment. This adventure also will make you a much stronger, happier, and wiser human being. Read on and let me share with you some things I learned through my twenty years of trial and error to help finally bring this amazing dream of yours into concrete reality.

PART I

The Writing Life

Chapter One

The Life of a Writer with a Full Time Job

I fell madly in love with writing the day I discovered it was possible to move people with words. In my younger days I was extremely quiet and shy and writing became an important emotional outlet. As early as I can remember, there has been this aching inside of me to tell a story. As the years have progressed, this deep desire to tell a story has become a lifelong obsession to polish and perfect my craft. For almost two decades I have been juggling a full time job while writing books, poetry, and freelance articles. Although my goal has always been write full time, it's taken me much longer than I had ever anticipated.

I made the decision in my mid-twenties that I didn't want to make my living writing what someone else tells me to for eight hours a day, five days a week. I was afraid to lose my passion for this thing of beauty that I love so much. So I found a job that wasn't connected in any way with writing and continued to write after hours, on my own time. Throughout the next twelve years, I published a few children's books and collections of poetry while dabbling in short stories. I also was accepting regular commissions to do personalized poems for special occasions like weddings, anniversaries, and such. A steady stream of small triumphs including the James Thurber Treat Prize in 2005 for my fable, "The Heiress and the Pea" kept my dream alive. All the while, writing kept me sane. It is what kept me going through all of the many ups and downs of life.

Juggling a writing career and a full time job was manageable for a number of years. My fate changed around the time I began seriously working on my first novel. About three months into the writing of Alarm Clock Dawn, my day job became more stressful and began to require more hours. I quickly found out that to produce anything of value in the way of long-fiction required three to four hour blocks of time. When you factor in a full-time job and commuting, this didn't leave much time for anything else, including sleep. Luckily, I had an abundance of vacation time built up at work so I started taking week long blocks of time off to work on the novel uninterrupted. The freedom to structure my days as I pleased is one of the best gifts I have ever given myself. I crafted my ideal daily writing schedule and learned so much about the rhythms of my creative muse and even how to coax creativity when it waned. In regard to the latter, walking our dog in the fresh air never failed.

As my writing vacation came to a close, I always found myself feeling frustrated and depressed about having to put the freedom of this writer's life back on the shelf again for an undetermined amount of time. I had this story locked inside of me that I wanted desperately to share with the world but my current life as it was didn't allow me the time to do it. These weeks of writing were only a tease. They gave me only a taste of the ambrosia that I had been working so many years to achieve and only fueled my fire to transition from my day job even more.

This decision I made long ago to exist with a foot in both worlds has provided me with some of my greatest joys, as well as some of my deepest sorrows. I am grateful for the fact that I can afford to eat, all of my bills are paid, my wife and I enjoy at least one vacation per year but there's no doubt that my existence in each world has suffered due to this balancing act. Because I always felt as if my big break in writing was always just around the corner, I never focused on pursuing a career path in my daytime job. Ironically, I suspect that my writing career didn't progress as quickly as it might have because I didn't always devote the time or energy to necessary to make it fully blossom.

After finally publishing my first novel, Alarm Clock Dawn, in April of 2013 and as I began to write the sequel, Truth Is Stranger, there was a distinct quickening. My day job began to demand even more of my time, now fifty to sixty hours per week. I found myself much more tired than I should have been at age forty-two. It was almost as though the Universe was reminding me that, to achieve the kind of writer's life I wanted, it was time to choose between being a "lifer" at my day job with a regular paycheck and benefits or the writer's life. My readership on social media was growing exponentially and I was presented with the wonderful opportunity to write this book that you're reading today. I was right on the cusp of something big, I could feel it.

It was at that precise moment that I decided to stop leaving so much of my future up to fate and rearrange my life to be more conducive to achieving the writer's life I so desired. I began a conscious effort to redesign my life, and the pieces began to slowly fall into place. First, to allow more time to produce quality writing I realized that I needed a job that demanded less energy and hours. Although it took a few months, eventually I found a job that was perfect for this stage of my transition, it required less of my time and wasn't nearly as stressful as the one I had before.

Even though my current job fits my situation right now, I make it a point to remind myself every day that it's only a stepping stone and not to allow myself to get too comfortable. I now know that achieving my ideal writer's life is the only thing that will bring complete satisfaction to my soul. I'm thankful for my day job but there's absolutely no room in my dream for spending eight hours of my day in a cubicle working for someone else. There's something highly attractive about working according to my own schedule and having the freedom to get up from the writing desk to take the dog for a walk if the mood strikes me. In two years from now, my plan is to have fully transitioned out of my day job and I have set clear goals to achieve this.

My advice to writers who are contemplating a similar path is to be very honest with yourself about the kind of life you want to achieve. If you wish to write full time, you simply must set pragmatic goals of how and when you wish to accomplish this. Your plan of action must be your top priority, because time moves swiftly. Ask yourself first, where would you like to be in six months, in a year, in two years? Then it is just a matter of plotting a step-by-step course to get there. Leave as little to chance as possible. To chase after the writer's life without a concrete plan is a costly mistake that is likely to end in wasted years, frustration, and sorrow.

If you have that aching deep inside of you to tell a story, you must kindle the fire of that passion and treat this gift of writing with the respect that it deserves. I guarantee you will make mistakes, but they're not mistakes if you learn from them. Each time you stumble, dust yourself off and continue to hone your craft. Network with others in the business and keep pursuing your passion. If you stick to this course, one day you will get the great privilege of telling your story and the world will know your name. Behind the story of every great writer is a little smarts, a fair amount of luck and a lot of persistence.

The path to achieving a healthy balance on the journey to attaining the writer's life consists of three elements: 1. A day job that provides a comfortable salary with adequate benefits but isn't overly time consuming or mentally draining; 2. Sufficient time to produce quality writing;

and 3. A fair amount of time for a personal and some kind of social life. Finding the right mix of these three aspects that work for your own unique situation will allow you to achieve success as a writer much more quickly. Fine tuning this formula until you achieve the proper balance can be very frustrating at times but keep in mind this is only a means to an end. If this path to becoming a full time writer is approached with clear goals and discipline, it will provide a more effective and comfortable life than the traditional starving artist strategy.

Chapter Two

What I Learned From Writing My First Novel

The unfinished manuscript for my first novel, Alarm Clock Dawn, sat on the shelf for years before I gained the confidence to begin a serious effort to complete it. In late 2010 I was working a full time job and publishing smaller works of poetry, short stories and children's books. I was a poet at heart and the novel was a pet project of mine, a Herculean task I didn't think I could ever accomplish.

The catalyst for this final push to finish the book was sparked by a single question from a friend at a party, "Have you finished that novel yet?" It wasn't so much the question that kindled the fire within me but it was how it was phrased.

The question was asked almost jokingly, in a way that made me think she didn't think I would complete it. I've since thanked her profusely for asking me that question because it made me take finishing the book more seriously.

So how has writing my first novel has changed me? It's taken my writing career to the next level. Novelists do get a certain amount of respect. It's not a fallacy; I've found that writers and non-writers now take me more seriously after I finished this first book. Although at times it feels like my dream of being a full time writer is materializing in slow motion, it is definitely coming true.

Another thing that finishing a novel taught me is that I'm a better and more disciplined writer than I thought I was. The voice of self-doubt isn't nearly as loud since finishing that first book. I'm working on the sequel, Truth Is Stranger. I have no doubt that it will be finished. With this second book writing a novel has become more of a formula to me. Write for a certain number of hours, finish a certain amount of pages. National Novel Writing Month offers an excellent template for us to follow. If you want to finish writing an average size novel in a month, you must write an average of two thousand words per day. Granted, two thousand words per day isn't feasible for most writers, but if you stretch the process out over six months, three hundred words per day could be accomplished by almost anyone with the desire to do so.

Completing my first novel was more difficult than I ever imagined. I won't sugar coat it, working on the manuscript those last few months was how I imagine military bootcamp to be. It has a way of breaking you down only to rebuild you into a more resilient person. The process of writing a novel stretches you past so many of your perceived limitations. For me, the beginning and the ending of the story were always clear but I struggled with how to connect the two. I simply learned that it's a necessity to plant yourself in that seat and get it done. I'm a much better writer for having had the persistence to see the process through.

Writer's block can be conquered. Some days I had no idea what I would write about and didn't feel like writing after working all day. What I learned is something I'll take with me for the rest of my life. Writer's block doesn't have to significantly delay a project. After a while, I learned that I had control over my creative mood and it could be easily sparked given the right environment. For me, it's like opening the channel. Once your brain is in tune with this channel of creativity, the words just flow. Some of my best writing has been accomplished after I felt like I couldn't write another word.

The level of satisfaction is incredible. Alarm Clock Dawn took a total of eight years from concept to completion. Finishing this book was one of the best days of my entire life. My wife and I dropped everything the day I wrote the last word on that last page and we went out to celebrate. I wept. Seriously, I did and I'm not usually a crier.

I live much more in the moment now. The level of concentration and attention to detail required to write a novel has really changed my perception of the world and even the quality of my inner dialogue. I realized this while taking my beagle for a walk shortly after I finished the manuscript. Colors pop, smells seem stronger, sounds more melodious. My whole life experience is richer because I tend to keep my consciousness more, "in the moment" and notice more of everything that is unfolding around me. I have been a serious meditator for nearly twenty years and writing the novel only enhanced the benefits attained from meditating for all those years.

I'm more humble. I'm in awe of the fact that my mind created a whole world. I will be forever grateful that the circumstances in my life realigned to allow me to finish that first book. I'm also thankful for all of those people in my life who supported me and believed in me throughout the grueling process. I'm sure so many people grew weary of hearing about the story.

I feel a stronger connection with and empathy for other writers. This is incredibly demanding work, especially as an amateur who has to work a full time job to pay the bills. To put the hours and dedication into something that isn't ever guaranteed to be a success takes a lot of belief and faith. I now feel an unbreakable bond with those who have ever accomplished it, both past and present.

The process of writing a novel is addicting. After finishing the book and realizing that I have the chops to do it, I'm officially addicted. Completing and publishing a novel is like what I imagine the first hit of potent drug to be like. Throughout the writing process, there are incredible emotional highs and, at times, devastating lows. The emotions experienced during the process of writing a novel mirror real life. It is gritty, it isn't always perfect but it sure is real.

Finishing a novel isn't the end, it's only thing beginning of a new and incredibly exciting path and much more work. For the project to be successful, you have to do book signings, appearances and marketing of any and all kinds to get yourself out there any way you can. With social media, it's not all that difficult to gain a following as a writer but to translate these followers into sales still requires an incredible amount of energy and creativity.

I'll be doing this the rest of my life. I still write poetry and essays but I know that nothing will ever compare with writing a novel. My second book, Truth is Stranger, is going to be much more layered and character driven. I can see I've grown but realize I still have much to learn. Hemingway is quoted as saying, "We are all apprentices in a craft where no one ever becomes a master." Only one book into my career as a novelist, I realize how much truth and wisdom drips from Hemingway's words.

Chapter Three

What is Your Definition of a Successful Writing Career?

Success can be defined in many ways. When I began on the path of becoming a published author two decades ago, I thought there was really only one option, to get published by a traditional publisher, sell a few hundred thousand books and be a success! When I first began my writing career, I had this vague and antiquated idea of where I wanted to steer my writing career. All I knew is I wanted to be accepted by one of the big New York publishing houses and become the next great American writer. I didn't have a clue as to what I was going to write or how I was going to get my work published. When I was twenty-one years old, I wanted to sell my first book to a major publisher, live in a big house, be famous and travel all over the world.

I look back at my younger self and have to laugh at how immature and loosely defined my vision of success was, but this is all part of life's journey. Each mistake, every bad decision you make only counts as a failure if you don't learn from it and change your approach the next time. Now I realize that one of the main reasons it took me so long to effectively launch my writing career was because I simply failed to define my vision of success in the beginning.

Success for me now means being able to write for a living and most importantly, having the freedom to live every day of the rest of my life on my own terms. Becoming ridiculously wealthy no longer figures into the equation for me because I've discovered what makes me truly happy is the process of writing itself, not the money and most certainly not the fame. Besides, you will learn as I have, if you wholeheartedly pursue your passion, the money will eventually follow.

Today with the multitude of high quality options for self-publishing paired with the true miracle of social media, success is within reach for many more authors. Still, I feel the biggest stumbling block for most creative people is to not invest the time and brainpower necessary to define what success means to them.

Ask yourself, would you like to be on the New York Times bestseller list, write as a hobby for extra income, or something in between? In the very beginning of your journey, or wherever you are on your path, take the time to decide what success means to you. Write this down and put it in a place where you'll see it every day, hold this definition of success in your mind with a clear vision. You can't arrive anywhere in life without first knowing where you would like your destination to be. This doesn't mean your definition of success can't evolve at some point later in your journey, it most definitely will.

How do you know you're getting closer to achieving your vision of success? You know you're getting close when your reality begins to resemble your defined vision of success and, believe me, you will instinctively feel it. Each time you achieve a goal or reach a new plateau in your writing career the nagging voice of insecurity begins to get more hushed until it eventually disappears altogether.

For me, I knew it came after I self-published my first novel. The process of writing that first novel was an emotional rollercoaster and many times I was filled with fear and self-doubt. I had no idea what I was doing and wanted to quit more than once. I was working an extremely demanding job during the day and finding the time and energy to write wasn't easy. After almost a year I had a finished draft and it was one of the most satisfying days of my life. During these eleven months, I discovered a secret. Every time I pushed past fear and self-doubt, it was as though the universe opened another door for me and whatever answer I needed somehow magically appeared. Try it, it's true.

Finishing the manuscript was only the beginning. Feeling the incredible rush of positive reader reviews were the icing on the cake. Throughout the book launch and first year after the release of my novel, I've discovered that my readers are my boss, I work for them and earning their respect is the most important thing to focus on. With my novel, I found my niche audience and it was them who helped to extinguish all remaining doubt that I was a real author. This entire experience was so gratifying and humbling, my readers will always mean the world to me.

Wherever you are on your journey, the best

thing you can do for your writing career right now is to pause and reflect upon what your own unique vision of success is. Hold this vision in your mind until it's so real you can smell, feel and taste it and then work backwards from there.

Chapter Four

Is Self-Publishing A Good Fit For You?

If you wish to be published by large traditional publishing houses, often you'll need to be represented by a literary agent before they will even look at your manuscript. The exception to this rule is in the Science Fiction and Fantasy genres, as most publishers will consider manuscripts in these genres without an agent.

This presents a problem for first time authors, because most agents will only accept authors with a track record of being published. If your work gets accepted by one of these large publishers for review, it will likely sit on a pile of other manuscripts anywhere from six to eighteen months before it's reviewed. If the publisher decides they are interested enough in your work to take a chance on you, you can count on another year to three years before your book is in the hands of readers. This path can be incredibly long and arduous.

Independent publishers, (also referred to as small presses or indie publishers) as their name implies, are smaller, with annual sales of no more than fifty million dollars in the United States. Most publishers in this category do not require the author to be agent represented but often cater to a niche readership. If you decide your project is a good fit for this type of publisher, it's wise to check the reputation of publishers you're considering on the website Pred-Ed.com (Predators and Editors).

The third option is self-publishing. It seems that every day more authors are choosing this path for a variety of reasons. Unfortunately, this path isn't easy either. One of the main positive aspects of self-publishing is the time between a finished manuscript and getting your book launched is greatly reduced. To generate respectable sales numbers with a self-published book, an author must wear every hat, they must be the writer, marketing director, accountant, editor, and the graphic designer. The level of responsibility can be daunting but you don't have to be an expert in any of these fields to get started, you need only to have a desire to succeed and the willingness to learn.

If you know you lack skills or have no interest in a particular area it's always possible to enlist the help of a person, or a team of people, who specialize in the areas that you lack in. Also, decide if you want to self-publish exclusively or eventually try to attract a literary agent or traditional publisher with your impressive self-published sales results.

Do you want to produce your book in hard copy format, eBook or both? Many people will tell you there are countless reasons to produce your work in eBook format only, but that can be a mistake. I've found that my main reader demographic, people aged 35-55, still very much prefer to read a traditional book. Sales of the paperback version of my novel have far exceeded what the eBook version has generated. The eBook version has still been useful for international sales because people don't have to pay for shipping. The other attractive aspect of an eBook is they can be given away for free during your online book promotions. The number of people who buy eBooks will surely grow with time as more people purchase tablets and eBook readers. For these reasons, I would encourage you to create an eBook version of your book no matter what the demographic of your readership is.

There are many companies out there who specialize in self-publishing and will do it without charges upfront, and I chose Lulu. It's very important to find the right fit for you. Make a short list of three of your favorites and take the time to heavily research each of them. The Preditors and Editors website is a great place to start. Read reviews online, peruse author message boards to get real world feedback on all of them as well before making your decision. Don't opt for extra marketing, cover design or editing services from your publisher. Hire individuals to do this, they will do a better job and will give you the same caliber of work, or better, for less money.

Self-publishing doesn't mean you don't have to spend money on the design and marketing of your book. If you have a limited budget, the eBook route is the way to go, but even with an eBook you can expect to spend at least a thousand dollars or more for a professional looking book. In my experience, graphic design and professional editing are the two most important places to spend your initial book budget dollars.

I can't stress this enough, people really do judge a book by its cover. It must be eye catching and legible as a tiny thumbnail because this is how readers will see it in online stores. Unless you're a graphic designer, I would advise hiring someone to do your cover for you. Check with your local art school, many times they have a huge pool of talented individuals who are eager for work and projects to add to their resumes.

It really took the incredible power of social media before self-publishing became a lucrative alternative to traditional publishing. I had self-published several books before my first novel in 2013 and they were only mediocre successes. Social media sites like Facebook and Twitter now allow a self-published author with a small budget to have incredible outreach for very little money. Promoting your projects this way still takes work and ingenuity to build a fan base on social media and it won't happen overnight. If you pay attention to what gets engagement on social media and continue to pour your energy into material that generates a response from your readers, over time you will eventually find your audience and earn an army of loyal readers.

The beauty of self-publishing is that authors don't need to clamor for the attention and approval of some publishing executive they've never met. Another wonderful thing is the direct connection with your readers. This direct connection with your audience allows almost instant feedback on your writing and it can teach you valuable lessons that will make you better at your craft.

As I mentioned, self-publishing is not an easy task and is very time consuming. For this reason, at some point in your career, you may discover that it may be easier and necessary to get the attention of a traditional publisher and you may decide to venture down that path. I'm almost to that point in my writing career now. After the release of the sequel to my first novel, I am going to have to seek traditional publication for my series of books. I am finding that to reach my goal of producing a new novel every twelve to eighteen months I'll need to sell the rights to my trilogy of novels to a major publisher that offers an advance. The author Hugh Howey has proven that it's possible to make the transition from a self-published author to a traditionally published author. He signed a deal with a major publisher and a contract for film rights for his "Silo" series of novels that were originally self-published in eBook format for the Kindle. His deal afforded him the best of both worlds as he retained his rights to sell his books online exclusively.

If I'm fortunate enough to make the transition to a traditionally published author, I will never forget the many joys and lessons learned during my years of self-publishing. No matter what, I never want to lose the direct connection I've so painstakingly forged with my readers. There is nothing quite like logging onto my social media accounts and getting direct feedback from someone who your writing has made an impact on or someone you can help over a stumbling block in their writing career. When you have experienced this direct connection, it quickly becomes apparent that, as writers (and readers), we're all really one big crazy, creative family and all of us are in this together.

Chapter Five

Achieving Work-Life Balance By Finding Your Ideal Writing Ritual

It takes an incredible amount of drive to become a successful author. It can often seem like a writer must have a dedication that borders on obsession in order to become successful. For this reason it is so easy to let your desire to become a successful writer consume your entire existence. However, just like any other career it is important to eventually find the balancing point between your personal and professional life. You must make time for the other things you enjoy in life and the people you love. History books are filled with writers who suffered because they failed to seek and achieve life balance. Unfortunately, many times these writers turned to unhealthy options like drugs and alcohol and ended up troubled souls. It's perfectly natural to be consumed with your writing while you're working but don't let writing consume your entire life.

Actually, your writing will benefit when you achieve the proper work-life balance. The quality of your writing becomes exponentially better when you experience life deeply. It's okay to make time for family, friends, and fun. While writing, if you feel yourself working from a place of desperation or have a difficult time pulling yourself away from your writing desk, pause and think of taking the time to enjoy life as field-research for your writing. If you do nothing but write all day, your writing won't reflect the richness and complexity of someone who has had real life experiences. I learned this important lesson many years into my career while writing my first novel, Alarm Clock Dawn. Real life provides you with an inexhaustible cast of characters and scenes that are better than you could ever dream up on your own. So travel, go to that party, spend quality time with your significant other. Your readers will thank you for it.

Making the most out of each and every writing session is a great way to make sure that you have sufficient time left over for everything else in your life. One easy way to work towards achieving a greater level of efficiency and inner satisfaction in your writing is to find your own unique writing ritual. Find a writing ritual that works with the natural rhythm of your body, mind and unique spirit. Many writers eventually settle into their own ritual through months or years of struggle, frustrating bouts of writer's block and inner turmoil. If you purposefully recognize and hone your own writing ritual from the beginning of your career it will gel much more quickly, your work and your personal life will be better for it.

I stumbled on an easy way to hone my own writing ritual while working on my first novel. I decided to give myself the gift of one week. I took five consecutive days of vacation time from my day job to experience what it's truly like writing for a living. I realize that vacation time is precious but giving yourself the gift of this week will be a great investment in the future of your writing career that will pay wonderful dividends. Your future is worth it! This one week of treating your writing as if it were your day job will give you a glimpse of what it's like to live a writer's life. By the end of that week, you should have a pretty good idea if you have the discipline required to do it.

During this week it should be your goal to:

Craft Your Ideal Work Schedule

Each writer is different, some of us are early birds, some of us are night owls and there are several variations in between. I'm an incurable early bird and was lucky enough to find my ideal writing ritual quickly while working on the final draft of my first novel. I usually rise at between 6:30 and 7:00, shower, eat breakfast and find myself at the writing desk by 9:00AM. I discovered that what works best for me is to divide the day into two shifts, three to four hours of writing in the morning and another two to three hours in the afternoon with a break for lunch in between. If I don't feel particularly productive at some point in the afternoon shift I allow myself a break to take the dog for a walk or go for a short bike ride. If I find my creativity stalling, physical activity and fresh air will almost always get the ideas flowing again. Be cognizant of when and how you produce your best work then simply start creating a time schedule for your writing within those parameters.

Create Your Writing Nook

The process of writing is sacred in its own right and should feel that way to a writer. Writing is a transformational act of self-expression that most writers also wish to one day pay their bills and put food on their table. It's very important to treat this magical process of creation with the respect it deserves and design an environment that helps to encourage your creativity to flourish. If possible, you should have a space in your home set aside for nothing but your writing. It doesn't have to be big or fancy but it should be comfortable and free from distractions.

My writing nook is on the second level of our house. My writing space is a small, secluded attic filled with natural light. After working in this space for a few writing sessions, I began to discover that the creative mood was enhanced merely by sitting down at the desk. Before I write, I make sure that my smartphone is across the room. Although I run my plethora of social media and author website from my phone and it's an amazing tool, I want no distractions during my writing session. I write on a laptop computer so

I also make it a practice to never stay logged into my social media accounts when I'm working on a manuscript.

It's important to keep your body comfortable while working so nothing pulls your attention away from your work. I have a standard office chair and a table that are ergonomically correct. I also have a small space heater nearby during the winter months, this keeps my fingers from going numb so my keystrokes have a better chance of keeping pace with my flow of ideas. A warm mug of my favorite green tea is typically within arm's reach. Sometimes I'll burn incense or play relaxing music.

Once you seek balance in your writing life, you will soon discover that the personal and professional aspects of your life will each become better and the creative process will start to blossom and feel as natural as breathing. You were born to tell your unique stories and the wellspring of creativity inside of you is just waiting to be tapped. These words are aching to be released and will begin to flow freely from your mind if only given the proper environment and mood.

Chapter Six

Things That Will Bring You Back To The Writing Zone

The sometimes elusive, "writing zone" is a small bandwidth of consciousness that exists in the creative mind when we're at our peak of creativity. For our creativity to be at its peak, we must be as healthy, in both body and mind, as we can be. We've all read about the well-documented exploits of famous writers and how they used drugs, alcohol, and even caffeine to fuel their creativity and get into, "the writing zone" but this almost never had a good outcome. I've found there are many positive and healthy choices that writers can make to enhance our creativity without the negative repercussions.

Science has proven that adequate sleep is vital to the proper functioning of our bodies and minds. Something as simple as getting the proper amount and quality of sleep can make the difference between a productive writing session and sitting for hours staring at a computer screen or blank piece of paper. People have different sleep requirements and preferences. I prefer to go to sleep well before midnight and rise early and I need at least seven hours, ideally eight hours of sleep, to function at peak efficiency. If I get less than that, it's futile to try to write anything of quality.

Sometimes it's not always easy to get the proper amount of sleep but we can take measures to ensure the quality of our sleep is the best it can be. I try to lay down and read a good book for at least fifteen minutes before I fall asleep, this usually always relaxes me. When it's time to fall asleep, I make sure the bedroom is dark and quiet (except for the white noise of a fan, or humidifier in the winter). It's also a practice to make the bedroom a, "No Electronics Zone" limiting the use of phones and tablets while in bed. These devices can easily cause us to lose track of time. I mean, who hasn't been sucked into Facebook or Candy Crush and felt that rush of adrenaline when they realized it's almost one A.M. and the alarm will be going off in four or five hours?

One of the best tools by far that I've found to enhance both writing and well-being is meditation. In my experience, most creative people are sensitive to begin with but meditation will deepen this sensitivity. I first incorporated meditation into my life twenty years ago when I was suffering from anxiety and depression. Meditation played such a huge role in allowing me to overcome these afflictions that I wrote a book about it. I feel that meditation is the ultimate key to healing us and allowing us to become more than we are. I promise you that a simple ten or fifteen minute daily meditation routine will make you a better writer by strengthening your ability to focus and access an inexhaustible source of creativity that exists within you.

The act of meditating brings you more in tune with the subtleties of your soul and the environment around you. The results aren't immediate but they will undoubtedly appear, you must only have a little patience and regular practice, even if it's five minutes per day. There are many resources out there, both online and in book form, to teach you the practice of meditation. Different styles and techniques of meditation work for different people but the most important thing is getting started in your search to discover what works best for you.

Many writers, such as Phillip Roth and Kay Ryan, have shared that they find exercise a necessary component to fuel their creative spark. I use different types of exercise for different reasons. If I have writer's block, I typically go for a walk or work in the garden. The simple and relaxing act of walking has a way of resetting my mind and the ideas always begin to flow again. Gardening also never fails to reconnect with my vein of creativity. There is something about immersing yourself in the natural world that helps to clear away the negative thoughts and feelings. It gets you right back into creative mode again.

It's almost impossible to write anything of quality when we're feeling stressed or worried for any reason. When I'm in this uneasy frame of mind, I use yoga or tai chi to calm myself and coax me back into the creative mindset again. I rely on yoga and tai chi DVDs but if you prefer the support of a group setting you can always check into regular classes in your area. These modes of exercise also have the added benefits of helping to alleviate the soreness and stiffness associated with one of the pitfalls of being an author, sitting for extended periods of time.

If you're feeling particularly lethargic or mentally exhausted and feel like you can't possibly write another word, cardiovascular exercise works better than caffeine to boost your energy and improve your mood. Mind you, it takes discipline to want to start anything strenuous when you feel like your energy is depleted, but it works without fail. If I'm feeling particularly blah and under a tight writing deadline, I'll hop on my bike and take a strenuous ride or walk for twenty to thirty minutes on the NordicTrack. After a few minutes of this kind of exercise, I'll usually need to stop and jot down ideas on my iPhone. I've written volumes of poetry this way. It's important to start your writing session immediately after your exercise routine while your creativity is at its peak.

Cardiovascular exercise can also be a useful tool for those writers who have an overabundance of energy. I often find it difficult to write if I haven't been able to expend enough energy, especially if the weather is particularly nice outside. I'll sit at the computer with my legs bouncing with my mind unfocused and racing in a million different directions. When I feel like a child trapped in a classroom when he'd rather be on recess, I allow myself a break and will take that bike ride or will cut the grass and then after I'm done I come back to the computer ready to work. The time I take to expend the energy almost always pays off in writing that truly satisfies my soul.

The key is to become more in tune with your body and mind and then find a form of exercise that you enjoy. Then you must learn when and how to use these tools to your advantage. Any form of cardiovascular exercise that increases your heart rate for an extended amount of time will boost your body's endorphins naturally. You will find that when used in the proper way all of these activities will help you to get in the mood to fill up those blank pages in no time.

Chapter Seven

Ways To Stay Motivated To Write

With the many distractions and responsibilities in every writer's life, it's easy to keep the dream of becoming a successful author categorized in that notorious mental folder we all possess, labeled "Some Day." Finding the motivation to write when you're juggling everything that life throws your way can seem daunting. You have to have an extreme amount of discipline and optimism to make the pursuit of a writing career work on a long term basis but it can be done. Following are a few ways to keep you motivated.

Remember what you feel like when you're not writing. If you're anything like me when I'm not writing I'm listless, I feel like my dream is slowing slipping away with each and every tick of the clock. The longer I go without writing the more anxious I become. I call this unhappy state, "non writing-itis" and it's a truly uncomfortable feeling that can only be cured by one thing, sitting down and filling up a blank page with words.

Be sure to give your writing the time it deserves. Carve out as much time as you can afford to write. Schedule blocks of time and be highly protective of them. Most indie authors don't yet have the luxury of writing full time so you must make this time for yourself and have the fortitude to defend it. It seems everyone and everything conspires against you when you set aside time to work on your craft but you must be firm and make it clear that your writing is important and it is something you must do.

Educate the people in your life to respect your writing time because many times they, especially if not creatively inclined, simply don't know how important it really is to your happiness and wellbeing. I promise, sooner or later they will get the message. One of my biggest fears is being at the end of my life and not having fulfilled my goals as a writer. I realize there's only one person who can make sure this doesn't happen and only one person to blame if it does.

One thing I began to realize as I got into my late-thirties and forties is that time passes far too quickly. I had to learn how to make the most of my time if I wanted to be prolific enough to succeed in this business. Once I had a fair amount of writing experience under my belt it become easy to know how long a particular project would take. When you begin a writing project, whether it be an article, poem, short story, or even a blog post try to estimate the length of time it will take and set a goal for yourself to complete it.

Remember, good writing habits are your friend! When working on larger writing projects you must craft a regular writing routine. When working on novels I like to work 2 to 3 weeknights for 3 to 4 hours per session and 6 to 8 hours one day on the weekend. Set ambitious yet realistic writing goals for yourself or else you'll, all of a sudden, realize that weeks have passed since you've last written.

Surround yourself with creativity whenever possible. There's something very inspiring about being around other creative folks. After all, it's my belief that the only people who fully understand creative people is other creative people. We creatives seem to feed off one another's energy. Go to art fairs and local theatre. Find music that inspires you. For each of my novels I've found one album that I listen to almost endlessly while I'm writing. With my first novel it was the band Beirut's album, "The Rip Tide" and while completing my second novel I find I'm habitually listening to Beck's, "Morning Phase."

There's something inspirational about the right music and lyrics and it gets me into writing mode instantly.

One of the most important ways to stay engaged with the act of writing is to read books. Even if you don't consciously realize you're learning, you will learn something useful from every book you read. Stephen King said, "If you don't have time to read, you don't have time to write." I find this very much the case. Sometimes it takes only reading the right passage in another author's book to spark a whole succession of original ideas for your own projects, the creative mind is funny that way. It took me a long time to realize that reading good fiction begets writing good fiction.

Groucho Marx was quoted as saying, "If you're not having fun, you're doing it wrong." To write and write well, you have to develop a love affair with what you're working on. If you don't feel this kind of joy at least some of the time during a writing project then you're probably stuck in the wrong genre and you may want to try another.

When I was beginning my first novel I had no idea how to write fiction so it seemed frustrating and tedious but I later realized I felt this way because I was still learning the basics of the technique of writing long fiction. Once I had a basic knowledge of the mechanics of writing fiction, it became intoxicating to create an entire world from my imagination. When I started getting feedback from readers who enjoyed my work and realized how it impacted them, I was hooked.

Bathe yourself in optimism wherever and whenever you can find it. As I've said many times before the path to becoming a successful indie author isn't an easy one. If you're not careful, you can quickly find yourself swimming in self-pity, disappointment, and negativity. I often find inspiration by studying the success stories of others. There are countless examples of creative people who have risen from the grips of poverty to become wildly successful. For example, Tyler Perry went from suffering serial bouts of homelessness in the 1990's to becoming the incredibly successful media mogul he is today.

I also save inspirational quotes on my phone and regularly read them and even post them to my social media accounts to inspire others. When I need an instant dose of motivation providing inspiration to others is always a surefire way to raise my spirits. It quickly renews my optimism so I can keep working towards my goals.

Chapter Eight

Cast Aside Your Fears and Say Yes To Success

Writing is a solitary profession and writers are typically very introspective (read introverted) people and therefore are naturally apprehensive about sharing our work with others, meeting new people, participating in media interviews, doing book readings, author appearances, etc.

If you want to make writing your primary profession, you will simply not make it unless you're willing to trust in yourself and your abilities enough to begin facing these types of fears.

Overcoming your fears won't happen magically overnight, it takes work. It's perfectly acceptable to take baby steps towards reaching your goal of becoming the poised, professional author that you're meant to be, but you must be brave enough to take the first steps. I promise you that your confidence will grow each time you stand up to fear and in turn, fear will lessen its grip on you. Do all you can to nurture your self-confidence and it will blossom and grow in ways that were previously unimaginable. Every so often I realize I just accomplished something that would have paralyzed me with fear just a few years ago and all I can do is feel grateful and smile.

Sometimes we consciously or even subconsciously sabotage our own success because of our phobias. I was so shy that in High School French I chose to take a failing grade instead of getting up in front of the class to read an assignment. I was a great student and cared about my grade, but I let fear win and each time I allowed this to happen my fear became stronger. I beat myself up for a long time after this because I knew it that running from my fears was wrong and I knew that I could do better.

I continued to battle shyness and fear of public speaking through my freshman year of college. I always secretly envied anyone who could get up in front of a crowd to speak with poise and confidence because I thought it was easy for them. What I've learned as I've gotten older is most people who seem at ease and relaxed in front of a crowd are still nervous inside but have only learned how to control it through practice.

Trust me, almost everyone, including seasoned actors, musicians, and politicians with years of experience still occasionally battle their nerves before and during an appearance. These butterflies are natural, it's just a matter of learning to master yourself and your nerves. What is not natural is letting fear control you.

Promoting your writing gets easier every time you trust in yourself and your work enough to meet the challenge head on. I discovered the endorphin rush that comes after successfully attempting something like an author appearance, book signing, recording a YouTube video, or doing a media interview becomes a little addicting.

My first major milestone in public speaking happened a few years ago when a friend asked me to co-facilitate a meditation and relaxation seminar for employees of a corporation that we both worked for. He knew that I had written a book on meditation and wanted me to speak about what I had learned in my twenty years of practice and walk the audience through a few guided meditations.

I painstakingly prepared for that seminar, making flash cards for my presentation, carefully choosing the music that I would play during the guided meditation exercises. Even though I was anxious, I was able to keep my nervousness at bay and got through it. I was so thrilled to later find out that the audience provided glowing feedback for my segment of the class. Many people in the audience said I didn't appear to be the slightest bit nervous. This wasn't the way I felt inside while presenting but this experience bolstered my confidence making the next similar opportunity that much easier.

Bill Cosby once said, "In order to succeed, your desire for success should be greater than your fear of failure." and this quote couldn't be more true. Most things in life are just a matter of perspective, instead of looking at an opportunity to promote your book as something to dread and be nervous about you must begin to view these opportunities with enthusiasm. Look forward to and welcome success. View each chance to share your work in any way as a sacred gift that has the potential to take your career to the next level.

When you're in a new or uncomfortable situation and you feel your nerves getting the better of you ask yourself this: would you rather spend the rest of your life working for someone else in a profession that is your second choice or would you like to, finally, achieve your dream of writing for a living? Remember to choose carefully because there are not many things in life worse than regret.

Big breaks rarely come around and if you pass one up you never know when you'll get that next golden opportunity. I speak from experience when I say there is no greater feeling in this world than standing up to, and conquering, a long held fear. Once you do this, it has a way of changing you from the inside out. After a while you will discover you've been transformed into one of those people who meets new challenges with confidence and poise. You'll also very likely find you have a steady stream of exciting new opportunities to share your writing with the world.

Chapter Nine

Balancing The Books

The life of an Indie writer can be filled with uncertainties, for most people the largest of these uncertainties pertains to income. As a writer, instead of receiving a regular paycheck your payday only comes when you sell what you've written. Don't let this dissuade you from following your dream. The fact is there is no job that is completely safe in today's economy. No matter what your profession, job security is now a fallacy. Even after you've worked for a company for years you can find one day without warning that your job has been outsourced. Once we truly understand that risk is everywhere why not devote your time and energy to something you absolutely love? If the financial challenges of becoming a full time writer are what's holding you back from pursuing your dream, stop worrying and start planning.

For some people there's an innate romance associated with a writer's life but when you begin to think about it more practically it's easy for trepidation to sink in. I know how scary it can be, I've been in the workforce since I was fifteen years old and receiving a regular paycheck for almost twenty five years. As I'm preparing to make the transition into becoming a full time writer, I've done thorough research and have begun to retool my entire life to make the transition to becoming a fulltime writer less of a shock. You only have to stop thinking like an employee and start thinking like an entrepreneur.

Your odds of success as a full time writer will be much greater if you have a practical plan in place which includes concrete and realistic goals. First off, it's very easy to underestimate how much money you'll need to support yourself with your writing but it can be done. I have a huge amount of respect for authors who have figured this out.

As I was looking at my budget I decided the best way to start would be to determine how much money it would really take to make the transition into writing full time. I have always told myself that my magic number would be two year's worth of my current salary. If I could earn the equivalent of two year's salary from my writing then I would feel comfortable putting in my notice at work and finally take the leap of faith that I've been fantasizing about for years. Of course, the amount needed to put your plan into action will differ for everyone based on your lifestyle and current finances. The first step is to determine your personal number and write it down somewhere.

To aid in your transition it helps to deeply examine your life and decide what can be eliminated from your monthly budget as well as how you can maximize the revenue from your writing. Unless you have a lot of cash saved or an alternate source of regular income it's best to have a lean budget as you're making the transition into writing full time, at least in the beginning. Frugality is your best friend during the transition into the writer's life. This part came easily for me because I'm one of the few creative people I know of that are also very fiscally conservative. My parents love to tell the story of how when I was a young child I would save my allowance for months to buy a toy that I wanted only to decide the next day that I wanted the money back and I would return the toy to the store unopened.

I guess it's always really bothered me to hand over my hard earned cash for things that aren't a good value or something that doesn't add any real value to my life. I would much rather have money left at the end of the month to have wonderful life experiences like seeing new places and trying new restaurants than having my life cluttered with a bunch useless of things. When it comes to buying stuff I've rediscovered something our ancestors practiced out of necessity, research everything you buy and purchase the best quality you can afford, it's always less expensive in the long term. For example, it absolutely drove me crazy to spend twenty dollars on a pack of five disposable razor blades that lasted only a few months. Three years ago I purchased a Merkur brand safety razor for $30 and a pack of 200 blades for $20. I've only gone through half of the box of blades in three years. This one single purchase has saved me several hundreds of dollars so far.

As I was started striving to live my ideal writer's life, the first thing to be eliminated from the household budget was satellite television. I was spending over one hundred dollars a month for this service and only watched a handful of channels. As an alternative, my wife and I discovered the digital TV antenna and Apple

TV. Now we get over twenty free local channels over the air from the antenna and more content than we can watch on Netflix and Hulu for around sixteen dollars a month. The content on these streaming services isn't as current as cable or satellite television but it's worked out just fine because we're watching far less television and have more time for more important things. If we want to watch a more current film there's always the option of renting DVDs from Red Box for less than two dollars per movie.

If you really start to examine your life you'll be amazed at the number of creative ways you can find to lower your expenses. It's just a matter of taking a look at your own personal situation and deciding what you can live without. Some other suggestions to get you started are growing your own vegetables and canning for use later and shopping at thrift stores. I haven't owned a new car for years but save thousands by buying cars that are still in great condition but just a couple of years old. I also bike to work when weather allows.

Once you begin to analyze your situation, ways to save money will become very apparent. Ironically, you'll find that most of the cuts you make to your budget will come along with the fringe benefits of simplifying your life, improving your health, enhancing your creativity, and giving you more free time to do things like read and write.

The English writer, Brian Aldiss said, "A writer should say to himself, not, how can I get more money?, but how can I reach more readers (without lowering standards)?" It's important not to let financial concerns slow the progress or stall the enthusiasm of your writing career. Focus on writing, learning, improving, and taking chances. As you grow your career, your income typically will increase organically.

Even before you can make the full transition into your dream of writing full time, it's good practice to view your part time writing gig like the business that it is. Before your writing can pay all of your living expenses, the first step is to make your craft self-sustaining. By self-sustaining I mean, try to support all the expenses associated with your writing with proceeds from your writing. When you try this you will realize that supporting writing expenses from only your writing proceeds sounds much easier than it is. If you don't think outside of the box you may find yourself stuck in a cubicle.

I've found that launching a writing career takes a fair amount of two things, time and money. To make your work known to the world you must pay for things like marketing, professional editing, and travel to and from appearances just to name a few. If you can get to the point in your career where your writing is paying for itself you will be that much closer to achieving the dream of making a living with your words.

Since income as a writer can be so sporadic, it's important focus on diversifying your revenue streams as much as you can to make the most from your writing. Begin to think of different and creative ways your can market the same work. For example, I publish collections of my poetry in book form but I also sell the poems individually, matted on parchment paper. In doing this, I produce two different products and can profit twice from the same poems. Additionally, I offer a service where I will collaborate with clients to create a completely original poem for a gift or special occasion and by doing so can use my talent as a poet for a third potential income opportunity and the best part is I love doing all of them.

As an indie author, you're busy writing, so it's easy to overlook all the ways to profit from your work, and many writers often do. The first thing to focus on is making it as easy as possible for readers to find you and buy your work. It's important to have a page on your website or blog that list live links to where readers can purchase each of your published books. Regularly post a link to this page, with an attention-grabbing introduction on your social media sites. It's also imperative to choose the correct keywords on your pages so they show up in internet search results.

Whenever you have the opportunity to do personal appearances like book club meetings, readings or any event where you have the chance to make a face-to-face sale it's important to have extra books on hand and provide your readers the option of purchasing these books easily with a credit card. Companies like PayPal and Square offer reliable, easy to use, and compact credit card readers that plug right into your smartphone. Buy one of these credit card readers and learn how to operate it. Never be hesitant to wisely invest in yourself and in your career. According to a recent survey of BankRate.com, fifty percent of Americans admit they carry less than $20 in cash, and nine percent say they don't carry cash at all. Giving your audience the ability to easily pay with a credit card is a simple way to improve your sales potential.

Another great way to add another source of revenue is to monetize your blog through pay per click ad programs such as Google's AdSense. This service will embed ads in your blog that usually correlate, at least remotely, to products or services you're writing about in your blog post. Once you sign up for these programs you will get paid each time a reader clicks on an ad. You can even download the free AdSense app to your mobile phone to manage your account on the go. You won't generate much revenue at first, but it will grow as more readers begin visiting your blog. Although it's not typical, Google reports that some users are making tens of thousands of dollars per month off this program. Whatever you make, every little bit helps.

I can't stress this enough, just because you choose to pursue a writing career doesn't mean you have to be a starving artist, it only requires you to think differently and have the discipline to stick to a budget. Use your gift of creativity to discover new and different ways to get people to pay you for your work and be mindful of the money that you're spending. If you accomplish this balance, you will be well positioned to successfully support yourself with your words. More than ever before writers really do have control of their destinies. Utilize all of the tools at your disposal and you will soon see that reaching the goal of becoming a full time writer will feel every bit as amazing as you imagined it would be.

Chapter Ten

What I Wish I knew As A Beginning Writer

The writing bug bit me in tenth grade when I was given an assignment to write a short story. It was a comedy piece about taking my driver's test. The teacher read it aloud, the class laughed and I was hooked. Since then I've held a succession of jobs that have nothing to do with writing. Finally after eighteen years and the publishing of my first novel, "Alarm Clock Dawn" I'm close to my dream of writing full time. Why did it take so long? Simply put, I made many mistakes. If I had a time machine and I could go back and tell my twenty year old self ten things about writing this is what they would be.

Learn the fundamentals of writing before you even attempt a writing career. I cannot stress this enough, even if you feel that writing comes naturally to you, learn grammar and the mechanics of writing. Take classes, attend workshops or read books on your own. You will need to do so eventually and getting it out of the way first will save you much precious time.

Polish, polish, and polish. A piece is almost never done after the first draft is complete. I don't know how many times I've emailed or posted a piece online that I thought was done only to have a new idea come to me or find a typo in it later. My wife jokingly refers to me as, "the tweaker" but after you have some years of writing under your belt you know when a piece is complete and until it isn't the piece nags at you and you can't stop thinking about it.

Take feedback about your work from those who are close to you with a grain of salt. I'm not saying to discount it altogether but those who know you are emotionally connected with you to some degree and their opinions will be biased. Seek true advice only from those who have attained, at least partially, the level of success you want to achieve. Even a short conversation with a person such as this can spark a quantum leap in your writing career. I've experienced this kind of creative spark many times and each time it happens, it feels incredible.

Diversify. It's wise to create multiple revenue streams if you plan to make a comfortable living at writing. If you want to write books, also consider seeking freelance writing jobs and/or speaking engagements. It's also a great idea to establish yourself as an expert on what you write about.

Work to overcome shyness. Most writers I know, including myself, were at one time introverts by nature. You need to work to become more outgoing and be ready at any moment to speak enthusiastically about your work. Begin with baby steps and each time you step outside of your comfort zone, you will build confidence. You must become your own biggest fan and best salesperson. I've done things in the last ten years, like public speaking and radio/television interviews that would've terrified my twenty-year-old self. There is an incredible amount of competition out there for the attention of readers and it doesn't matter how good your work is. If it isn't getting in front of readers it will never get noticed.

A writing career is not easy. It's very easy to romanticize the writer's life but most times it is far from glamorous and, in fact, is one of the most difficult things you will ever do. To be a successful writer requires a mega dose of hard work, commitment, good networking skills, optimism, and also a healthy dose of luck. If you have the discipline to hone your craft writing can be equally as rewarding as it is difficult.

Beware of any publisher, agent or company asking for money from you to do business with you. There are plenty of unscrupulous individuals and companies out there who prey on both the vanity and naiveté of aspiring writers. Thankfully, reviews are now just a click away on the internet. Even if you are self-publishing your work, invest the time in reading online reviews before you sign a contract or upload your work.

Read voraciously. Reading the work of other authors will expand your vocabulary and will make you a better writer.

Develop your own unique voice and learn how to spark creativity. If you listen to the critiques and feedback of other writers too much, you will lose your own unique style or voice. Your style is what eventually will set you apart and allow you to develop your niche, which will ultimately develop into your fan base. Certain people say it's wise to force yourself to fill up a blank page every day to stay sharp. That doesn't work for me. If I encounter writer's block, I've learned it's best to take the dog for a walk, go for a bike ride or do anything that has nothing to do with writing and pretty soon the ideas start flowing freely again.

As writers, we don't choose to write, we have to write. Writing is not only a form of personal expression, it is therapeutic and it is also a lifelong journey of self-discovery. If I stop writing I feel there is a huge void within me, life doesn't seem as full filling. Twenty years into my career, I'm still learning new things and polishing my work with every project. Take your craft seriously, create a sacred space to write that is quiet and free from interruptions. Although writers spend lots of time crafting fictional characters, ironically, the act of writing develops the character of the author more than anything else.

PART II

On Writing

Chapter Eleven

Crafting the First Draft of Your Novel

So many writers, myself included, suffer from a great sense of impatience. Many of us are so busy chasing success that we fail to spend the time and effort necessary to master the fundamentals of our craft. Our writing isn't as sharp and polished as it should be and as a result, our writing careers don't blossom to their full potential.

With the advent of self-publishing and social media, authors have the option of publishing their writing instantly, whenever they want. This has many upsides but one huge downside is an abundance of second-rate writing. Gaining mastery of the basic techniques of the craft will take your writing from good to as great as it will need to be to make your career a success in this highly competitive business. You need to take that same enthusiasm you feel for sharing your writing, and apply that same zeal to fully mastering the techniques in which you tell your story.

I'm embarrassed to admit that, as with so many things in my writing career, I did this backwards. I didn't fully grasp the importance of mastering the fundamentals of writing fiction until I was laboring over the first draft of my debut novel, I was already many years into my writing career. You could say that I took the scenic route instead of the direct path. In the spirit of saving you from making the same mistakes I'd like to share a few aspects of writing fiction that were particularly challenging for me. In soliciting feedback from other Indie authors across my social media sites, many of them admit to having difficulties with these same issues as well.

DIALOGUE

Writing effective dialogue was, by far, the most difficult thing for me to learn. For dialogue to work, it must be as realistic as possible. Keen observation of the world around you will give you everything you need to know about this key element of crafting good fiction. Begin to pay attention to how people really communicate, including what they say and how they say it, their reactions to what others say, facial expressions, body language, and what they do with their hands. I've found one of the best places to study how people communicate is at a bar. There's something about the close proximity, combined with a few drinks that tends to open people up to relaxed and open communication. When my wife and I travel, we will often eat our meal at the restaurant bar. Not only do you get seated immediately but you usually meet extremely interesting people who will provide you with as much material for your writing as you need.

It's best to leave dialogue between characters simple and concise. Refrain from making a conversation between characters too lengthy as this almost always interrupts the flow of your story. Dialogue should be reserved mainly to convey key information and to reveal character. Remember, don't allow your characters to freely give away all that they're feeling. In real life, people are complex and your characters should be as well. Hold something back, your characters can reveal volumes about themselves by what they don't say or what they only allude to. Subtleties in dialogue, things that you leave out, will engage the reader's imagination in a way that allows them to participate in your story and begin to view your characters as real people.

You must learn to be a bit of playwright to

create truly engaging dialogue. When working on a scene, imagine your characters actually speaking the words you've written and to make it even more realistic, act it out with a group of friends or a writer's group. This is a simple and effective exercise to reveal bad dialogue. You must become the characters, get inside their skin, and learn how they would interact with others. Read every exchange of dialogue in your work aloud and polish it until it's believable and makes sense.

The proper use of dialogue tags really confused me. They are essential to fiction because you have to convey to your reader which character is speaking for your story to make sense. I first tried to learn how to use dialogue tags by reading other authors but it became confusing because writers use different styles and only made me more confused. My breakthrough happened when I participated in a short story workshop with C. Michael Curtis. He taught me the basics of using dialogue tags. What I learned from the workshop was that the only way to master writing dialogue is to practice. Most times tags should be kept simple, such as "he said" or "she said" but this can quickly become tedious to your reader so you have to mix it up.

I didn't fully master the subtleties of using dialogue tags to their full advantage until I was rewriting the first draft of my novel. What I learned was magic, you can use certain verbs in your dialogue tags to show emotion, you can use action to show which of your characters are speaking, and both of these will keep your plot careening forward. Here are some examples.

"You seriously want to do this?" he chuckled.

"You seriously want to do this?" he asked, chuckling.

Read each of the two lines of dialogue again, which of them is more effective? With just one minor change, the second line flows better and paints a picture in your head while you read it. This is your goal, to get your reader to paint that mental picture. This is how every writer of great fiction becomes an artist with their words.

You can also denote which character is speaking by utilizing the sentence before and after your dialogue instead of a traditional dialogue tag. This method eliminates the need for a tag altogether as in the following examples.

Johann crossed his arms over his chest and stroked his chin. "The strange thing is I believe them."

"What are you doing?" Seth glared over the top of his glasses.

This method of not using dialogue tags, when done sparingly can infuse much more emotion and detail into your story than a simple "he said" or "she said". It also helps to break monotony for your reader in sections of your story where there's a lot of dialogue. As you're rereading a section of your dialogue that feels flat and not keeping your attention enough, try using the "non-tag method" to help spice things up.

One last thing to remind you on the use of dialogue tags is to always make the first letter of your tag lowercase (e.g., "Can you get me a cup of water?" he asked.) This is another reason my editor is a saint. She had to remind me of this no less than twenty times. What she told me to make me remember was if you capitalize that first letter of the tag (e.g., "Can you get me a cup of water?" He asked.) it technically becomes two sentences instead of one. I've seen many beginning writers make the same simple mistake.

USE OF LANGUAGE

Many beginning writers, especially those who've also written poetry, tend to use overly flowery and descriptive language when writing fiction. It's good to remember what works in other genres doesn't always translate to fiction. Readers tend universally to connect with a simple and honest writer's voice. Use overly descriptive language only where you absolutely need to in your stories because it slows down the action and interrupts the flow of your story.

So many authors fail to choose their words carefully enough and their stories suffer because of it. You should increase your vocabulary and the best way to do this is by reading other authors. Reading is an essential part of becoming a good writer so be sure to allow yourself time to read the work of other authors. I used to believe that I would lose my unique voice if I read other author's fiction. This just isn't true. I found the key is to read a variety of other writer's work, this way you won't have to worry about picking up other writer's voices. You'll also improve your vocabulary and subconsciously enhance every aspect of your writing skills.

You don't need to prove your intelligence to the reader by using overly complicated words. It's best to use the right word in ways that create reality for the reader. Use descriptive words that pull your reader into the story. The rain doesn't just fall. Rain can also pelt, drench, drown, drive, hammer. Use your imagination to choose the proper words to add unique and memorable texture to your story.

PACING

Writing a novel is like running a marathon. You must pace yourself and take the time to develop your story being careful to reveal too much at once.

Pacing is very important to learn if you plan to write any work of fiction. Pacing is the technique of controlling the speed and flow of your story. Master the art of pacing and you will hook your readers. The easiest way I found to study how pacing works is to pay attention to how directors accomplish this in films. Pacing plays an important role in how your reader engages with your story emotionally. You'll notice the films that really draw you in are the ones that have fast pacing in the very beginning. This holds true for fiction as well. You typically will want to engage readers within the first few pages by the use fast pacing. Quick pacing also is important in the climax, and other more critical moments of your story.

Action is one of the most important ways to keep your reader engaged and turning the pages. I'm not talking about explosions and car chases, although these can have their proper place. By action, I refer to keeping the story moving swiftly and not allowing it to stall out. "Show, don't tell" is what my editor had to tell me over and over again while rewriting the faster paced scenes in my first novel. I would embarrass myself if I told you how many times my editor had to remind me of this.

Contrast between slow and fast pacing is very important to the balance of a good work of fiction. Slow scenes may not be as attention grabbing as fast ones but they are every bit as important. Think about it, if an entire novel was written using nothing but fast pacing, the reader would be exhausted and eventually they would become callous to the intensity of your climactic scenes. Slow and quiet scenes, in the right places, add variety to your story and also build momentum to those fast and high tension moments of your story. Slower scenes also help readers to become invested in your characters through character development. The roller coaster wouldn't be nearly as exciting without the painfully slow climb to the top of the hill just before the stomach churning plunge from the dizzying height.

What helped me to overcome the tendency to "tell" instead of "show" was to imagine each scene in the novel as it were being shown as a film on the big screen. This simple technique works quite effectively to remind you about the importance of using imagery to deepen the reality of your story. By using this method your words will paint a vivid picture in your reader's imagination that will temporarily whisk them away from their worries and cares and into the fictional world that you created. To me, a good piece of fiction is a twenty-dollar vacation that I don't need to pack a suitcase for. If I don't feel invested in a novel by the second chapter I'm not likely to even finish the book.

Ways to speed up your story:

- Shorter sentences and even the creative use of sentence fragments.
- Showing versus telling your story
- Emotional and dramatic dialogue
- Active verbs (not passive). An action verb is something that a person or thing can do. For example, "The teapot whistled on the

stovetop."

- Action and fight scenes
- Engaging the reader's senses

Things that slow down your story:

- Longer, more descriptive sentences
- Sharing character's thoughts
- Adverbs (many of these end in "ly" like abruptly and cheerfully)
- Telling your story versus showing
- Romantic and developmental scenes

CHARACTERS/CHARACTERIZATION

Good fiction is driven by characters. You must craft characters that are memorably unique and life-like. I commonly read stories where characters are lifeless and two-dimensional. The problem is that the authors are just scratching the surface and not using the full potential of their imagination. Remember, the good stuff is down deep. The poet Maya Angelou said, "I've learned that people will forget what you said, people will forget what you did, but people will never forget how you made them feel." This is very much the case when it comes to writing fiction. You have to make the readers *feel* the story to the point that they have a personal stake in the lives of your characters, especially your protagonist and antagonist.

A good exercise I used when writing Alarm Clock Dawn was to create a profile of each of the main characters before I wrote the novel, I spent the most time on the protagonist, Adam Harking and antagonist, Johan Pfizer. Fill up pages about the details of your characters, even search the internet and find pictures of people that most closely resemble your character and save these pictures in the character profiles you create. Spend time listing anything that helps to flesh out the character in your imagination.

The list of ideas to help you in this exercise is lengthy and includes your character's physical description, personality (include behavioral quirks), life history (including their family), life goals and motivations, fears, and even what they carry around in their pockets. Keep these character profiles on your computer or even on notecards so you can refer back to them often as you're writing. Your characters must become real to you before they can leap off the page for the reader.

It's very useful to expound on some of the details you craft in your character profiles by using them as a writer's prompt. Imagine your protagonist is being interviewed and is asked to explain their life story and write out the response. Another idea: The CIA has created a psychological profile of your antagonist, write about what it contains. When creating writer's prompts for the purpose of fleshing out your characters, you can pick any topic, like your character's life goals, fears, and main motivations. Use the scenes you create to learn intimate details about your characters. This shouldn't feel like drudgery to you, be creative and make it fun! Even if the scenes you create don't make it into your novel, the ideas certainly will. Investing the time to do these writer's prompts will make your characters more real to the reader.

It's important to create a mental picture of each of your major characters for your readers early on in your story. When you accomplish this each time they encounter that particular character the book the character comes alive in your reader's imagination. Each character should have things that make them memorable and set them apart from other characters in your story. There are many details that can make characters unique are physical traits, the clothes they wear, and even their scents. Scent is very much intertwined with human memory and imagination. Bear, one of the main characters in my novel, didn't wear deodorant. What could more memorable than excessive body odor? I spent so much time developing the characters in my novel they now seem like old friends.

WRITER'S VOICE

The writer's voice is defined as a combination of a distinct usage of syntax, diction, punctuation, character development, dialogue, etc., within a given body of text (or across several works). More simply, it's the unique way in which you use all the tools of the craft to tell your story. I'm a firm believer that a writer's voice isn't something to be developed as much as it is to be discovered. Just as each of us has individual personalities, deep within all writers is a unique voice waiting to be found.

Many beginning authors make the mistake of trying to mimic the style of their favorite authors. In doing this they cheat themselves and their readers because a unique voice is one of the things that will set you apart from the competition. There's only one way to discover your voice and that's by practicing. You must write on a regular basis and try not to overthink but rather let your voice come out organically. Once you've written a small body of work go back and reread them and look for patterns and similarities in the different pieces no matter the genre, this will offer clues to what your writer's voice is.

NARRATIVE VOICE

The narrative voice is the person who is telling the story in a work of fiction. When it comes to choosing a narrative voice there are enough options to make your head swim. So we don't get lost in too much detail, I'm only going to focus on two of most effective options in this chapter, first and third person narrative voices.

The *first-person narrative voice* is usually your protagonist or hero. There's a great advantage to this because it allows your reader to really get to know the protagonist of your story and will make them more invested in what happens to them. The story will seem more believable to your reader and is probably the easiest option for a beginning writer to master.

Third-person narration is different from first-person narration. The third person narrator is a character in the story who doesn't explain his or her role in the action. Some third-person narrators describe the story from a limited point of view; others, however, are omniscient.

-The *third person omniscient* narrative voice is when your narrator knows and all sees all, including what different characters are thinking and feeling. This can be useful because it allows you as a writer to explore different perspectives of the same events in your story.

-*Third person objective* is a neutral narrative voice that is an impersonal observer and reporter of what is unfolding in your story. With this voice, your narrator will never interject their personal opinions. As a result, your reader will be likely to forget that the story is being narrated at all.

-In the *third person limited* narrative voice a narrator reports the facts and interprets events from the perspective of only one character.

One of the biggest issues beginning writers face is shifting narrative viewpoint. This is only mastered with practice. A good rule of thumb is to write from the viewpoint of your chosen point of view character for the scene you're working on and you should stay on track.

When you take the time to develop this deep appreciation and respect for the fundamentals of your craft, it's as though you forge this unbreakable bond with all of the successful writers down through the ages. You will instinctively feel you have been accepted into their fold, you will know that you've earned your pen, and there will be no doubt in your mind that you are a real writer.

Chapter Twelve

Tips on Writing (and Completing) Your Debut Novel

I started my first novel, Alarm Clock Dawn, a full eight years before it was completed. I would work on the manuscript for a few days and then back up on the shelf it would go, for sometimes several months at a time. The complete concept of my novel was locked inside my head but didn't have the slightest idea of how to make the story come alive on paper.

I would sit down with every intention of writing but the session would invariably end unproductively and in utter frustration. Most of this frustration came from my lack of experience in the mechanics of writing long fiction. This self-defeating routine ended the very day I realized that everything you need to know to write a novel can be easily learned. The only thing truly holding me back in my mission to complete the book was attributed mainly to my impatience, fear of failure, and lack of confidence in my own writing abilities.

It might sound obvious but many writers, myself included, fail to learn the basics of how to write a novel before they attempt to start the creation process. I believe this is the precise reason why so many of us fail to complete our debut novel. I could go into some detail in regards to the mechanics of writing long fiction but to cover this in just a chapter or two wouldn't begin to do the topic justice.

If you have it set in your mind to write a novel,

chances are you already have some kind of idea of what kind of story you'd like to write but, in case you don't, my advice is to simply be mindful of the genres of books and films you're drawn to. The kinds of books you enjoy are a good indicator of the type of book you should write. To have the discipline to finish anything the length of a novel it really helps to have an intense interest in what you're going to write about. You must write from the heart, not what genre or topic is in vogue at the current moment. Make every effort to really get to know yourself as a reader and as well as a writer and it will quickly become apparent who your future niche readers are.

My advice is to look for novel writing workshops or classes in your area, if none are offered, there are some resources that offer online writing courses and some of these courses are even free. Again, Google is your friend, whenever there is something you need to learn, think in search terms. Plug in the search term, "Free Online Novel

Writing Courses" or a variation of this term into Google and you will be well on your way to finding what you need. Keep in mind that many colleges and community colleges offer great courses on writing a novel and many of these don't show up in Google searches. It's always a good idea to check for these courses on the individual website of the schools nearby.

A few workshops I've found will even allow you to use a manuscript that you're currently drafting as part of the class curriculum so you're learning the techniques while working on your own book. In terms of craft, you must master things like story architecture, fleshing out characters, plot pacing, dialogue, and scene construction to name a few. If you already have the seed of your novel locked inside your head the first instinct is to jump in and begin writing immediately. If this is your first novel and you've had no previous instruction on how to write long fiction I would encourage that you make an investment of six months (or less) in getting the proper education on how to write a novel, this small investment in learning technique save you much time and frustration in the end.

The average length of a novel today is 80,000 to 120,000 words. Many say anything shorter than 80,000 words runs the risk of be deemed too short. Yes, there's no denying it, the word count is daunting but it doesn't have to be. It's all a matter of perception and any goal this large should be broken down into manageable pieces.

November is National Novel Writing Month or NaNoWriMo, as it's more commonly known, offers just the formula you need. NaNoWriMo is like writer's boot camp and can offer you many of useful tools to get your book completed even if it isn't within their established timeline. As you might know, the goal of NaNoWriMo is to complete a 50,000 word book in a month. If you take a look at the math, you must write 1,667 words a day for the entire month to reach this goal. Visit and register on the website, "campnanowrimo.org" before you start this exercise, the website will allow you to track your progress and give you great support along the way. The great thing about the "campnanowrimo.org" website is that it can be accessed year round, not just in November.

The trouble for most of us who are juggling a full time job, a personal life, and writing is trying to conjure up the time to meet this lofty goal. The magic moment began for me when I realized that the "NaNoWriMo-police" wouldn't come to arrest me if I didn't follow their formula to the letter. You can easily stretch their timeline out for longer durations to suit your particular schedule.

Does writing 440 words per day seem a more attainable goal? This is the amount of words you would need to write per day to complete the first draft of an 80,000 word novel in half a year. Naturally, some days you'll write less, some days you'll write more, but if you stick as closely as possible to this 440 word per day goal, you will have a first draft in less than a year. Remember, no matter how large the goal it can be kept manageable if it's broken down into smaller pieces. Keep in mind this first draft will be far from a finished manuscript, and that's normal. Before it's ready for the public your book will require further editing and refinement but you will be just a few steps away from completing your debut novel.

After you feel the adrenaline rush of completing the first draft, pat yourself on the back and take time to celebrate. You will never forget completing the first draft of your first novel, it is beyond special and will never quite feel the same way again. After all, you can now call yourself a novelist.

At this point, I advise setting the manuscript aside for a few days and reading the entire thing

OUT LOUD, keep a pen handy to flag any typos and reword any awkward sections that you come across. It's also wise to hand it off to a group of volunteers or even a single individual you can trust to give you thorough and honest feedback. After the novel has been read aloud by you and looked over by people you trust, do the rewrite. If you're self-publishing, hire a professional editor to do the final polishing, the money spent on a competent editor will be a wise investment in your writing future.

Chapter Thirteen

Overcoming Writer's Block

Writer's block is one of the most frustrating afflictions that a writer can suffer from. It can cause unparalleled stress from project delays and missed deadlines. It can even cause you to second-guess your talent. It's safe to say that everyone has suffered from writer's block at some point in their lives. Studies have shown that under extreme stress the human brain shifts control from the cerebral cortex to the limbic system, which is the part of the nervous system associated with the fight or flight response. It's difficult to say if stress causes writer's block or vice versa but whichever comes first, writer's block can surely be conquered.

When I first began working on my novels, some days I had no idea what I would write about and didn't feel like writing after working all day. What I learned is something I'll take with me for the rest of my life, writer's block doesn't have to significantly delay a project. After a while I learned that I had control over my creative mood and it could be easily sparked given the right environment. Getting into the "writing zone" for me is like opening the channel, once the brain is tuned in to this channel of creativity the words just flow. Some of my best writing has been accomplished after I felt like I couldn't write another word. Following are some of my tips for getting your creativity back:

Try to find a space where all you do is write. The environment has to be comfortable and as free from distractions as possible. After a while merely stepping foot into that sacred space will help to coax your creative mood.

Create the mood with soft music, a candle or burn a mild incense. I usually play classical or New Age music but it's all a matter of finding what works for you. This will all help you to get your writing, "groove on".

Assess your frame of mind before sitting down to write. If you find your mind is full of other things, try this short meditation before beginning to write. Close your eyes, straighten your back. Breathe in deeply through your nose for a count of 5, hold for a count of 3, exhale through your mouth for a count of 5 (remember, 5-3-5). Repeat this 5 times. Each time you exhale, imagine the stress and worries of the day leaving your mind and your body. I know, it sounds deceptively simple but this is a powerful tool.

Remember, never judge your first draft too harshly. Just write. First drafts are never perfect but many times contain the seed of a great idea but, like a diamond in the rough, must first be cut and polished to reveal its many facets of brilliance. The more you remember this, the less anxiety you'll have.

When working on long fiction, outline your chapters first. Many people sit down and try to write a 60,000+ world novel while staring at a blank white screen or page and become overwhelmed to the point of being paralyzed. Create the framework first, then fill in the gaps, it's much easier.

When all else fails, walk away. Engage yourself in something else, anything other than writing. It might sound silly but walking the dog has freed me from the grips of debilitating writer's block. Usually after a few minutes the ideas begin flowing again, I've used my smart phone more times than I can count to record the ideas after the dam breaks.

Above all, believe in yourself and keep writing. Poet Sylvia Plath said, "The worst enemy to creativity is self-doubt." This is so true. As a writer, you will eventually look back and realize that you have become better with each word you've typed. In the end, it doesn't really matter if that particular writing session is good or bad, the most important thing is the act of writing itself. Write on!

Chapter Fourteen

Editing and Revising your Novel

Before a traditionally published book reaches the bookstore shelves it is often edited, revised, and rewritten several times. The work has only just begun when the first draft is done. Indie authors who are self-publishing should pay very close attention to this phase of their project to ensure their story reaches its highest potential. The editing and revising stage takes lots of patience and, I promise, does get easier with practice.

Many writers are confused by the difference between editing and revising. The two are very different. Both are essential steps to creating a finished manuscript that is ready for a professional editor. The first phase of this process, editing, refers to the mechanics of the craft such as typos, punctuation mistakes, inconsistency in tense (mixing past/present tense), and misused words. Revising is the second phase and involves word choice, content organization, and sentence structure. In the end, the revision process is intended to ensure that your story is clear but also compelling to the reader.

If you don't remember anything else from this chapter remember this, after your first draft is written, set it aside at least two weeks. The reason for this break is you've likely been working on your manuscript for months and if you start editing and revising now you'll read your story with writer's eyes. To be effective at editing and revising you'll need to view your story with a reader's perspective. After you've accomplished the awesome achievement of finishing a first draft, you should be celebrating for at least two weeks anyway. As I've said before, writing is demanding work so you must learn to celebrate each success.

Editing

After two weeks have elapsed, print out the manuscript and read it aloud to yourself. If you have someone else to read it, this is even better. Many times their expressions and feedback will give you an even deeper perspective on what is working in your story and what is not. Mark up the errors and trouble spots with a red pen, write notes and ideas in the margins. After two weeks, these trouble areas and errors should jump out at you. Once you have read the whole manuscript aloud, noted typographical errors, and problem spots, it is now time to rewrite it. Most authors use a computer these days so this just involves changing your original electronic document to match the markups you made in the printed version of your edited story. If you're one of the few writers who still use a typewriter or write in longhand, I'm sorry, but this rewrite is a necessary step.

Now we find ourselves precisely at the point where many beginning writers make a huge and costly mistake. They are itching to hand their work off to someone else to polish their story so it's ready to be published. I know how it feels, I was guilty of doing this with my debut novel (my poor editor). Resist every urge to be impatient at this stage of the game. Professional editors cost a lot of money and this is something most beginning writers typically don't have. It's best to work smart and not to have an editor spend their valuable time correcting things that you, or your beta readers, can discover and correct for free. Remember, time is money in the author-editor relationship. Before you hand your story off to a professional, it must be the absolute best it can be.

In terms of editing, pay especially close attention to consistencies in narrative perspective. The most common mistake I see writers make is using "you" when another viewpoint should be used. In a first person narrative, the narrator should be referred to as *I*. A third person narrative requires the narrator to be referred to as *he, she, it* or *they*.

Another common problem for many writers is the pesky past/present tense shift. For the sake of clarity, the verb tense in our writing must be logical. Following is an example of illogical verb tense shift.

As the taxi **approached**, the rider **steps** to the curb.

In the sentence above notice the word, "approached" is in the *past tense* while the second verb, "steps" is in the *present tense*. While the reader can understand what the sentence is trying to get across, these types of illogical verb tense shifts will distract and confuse. Even if the distraction is subconscious, it will interrupt the flow of your story and possibly prevent the reader from forming that all important mental connection with your story.

Here's the proper use of verb tense in the same sentence:

As the taxi **approached**, the rider **stepped** to the curb.

In the second example, both verbs are in the past tense. With just one small change, the sentence flows more smoothly. Nothing stands in the way of the action. Action is vital in fiction because it sparks the reader's imagination and pulls them into the story. Once you begin to view your story with reader's eyes you will realize that good fiction can be easily constructed sentence by sentence, scene by scene.

Revising

After the editing of your story is complete (typos, punctuation mistakes, inconsistencies in tense, and misused words) it's time to start the revision process. Before revising, print out a copy of the freshly corrected manuscript so none of the previous errors are there to distract you. It may feel like you're killing too many trees but the revision process is worth it, this is one of the most crucial steps in writing a good book. Now, read the entire story again as quickly as your schedule allows, ideally in no longer than a weekend.

As you're completing this second reading of your work, it's important to ask yourself things like:

- Is the story engaging?
- Does the story have the proper flow?
- Does your story have continuity?
- Is everything you're trying to convey in your story clear to the reader?

This last bullet point, clarity, will be impossible to determine on your own. The level of clarity you've achieved in your writing is best determined by feedback from beta readers. Beta readers are people you choose to read your story for plot holes, problems with continuity, characterization, and believability. I'll explain more about beta readers later in the chapter. If you've never used beta readers, you'll be surprised by the value they will add to your project. You will quickly learn that the variety of opinions and differing perspectives beta readers provide make them worth their weight in gold.

The most engaging novel I can think of is Harry Potter and the Sorcerer's Stone. I would guess that more adults went to work tired due to that book than any other in modern history. Who doesn't know someone who stayed up half the night because they couldn't put it down? J.K. Rowling made her characters extremely likeable, she infused the story with action, and included an intricate level of detail that brought such a sense of realism that the whole magical world comes alive!

In Harry Potter and the Sorcerer's Stone, Rowling endears the reader to Harry from the very beginning. As the story opens up with Harry living with an abusive aunt and uncle, you can't help but feel sympathy towards him. Shortly thereafter the gate to Rowling's magical world open as Harry receives letters from Hogwarts informing him that he's a wizard. From the first page, the flow of the story sweeps the reader, like a river, pulling them to smoothly to the end. Some scenes in the book are like white water rapids, leaving the reader breathless and exhilarated and in some scenes, the current slows down and causes them to become more introspective.

When revising your story it's very important to make sure it contains a high level of continuity. By continuity, I mean consistency in the details of characters, plot, places, things, and events in your story. All these things must be logical and in alignment to make your story believable to the reader. When dealing with writing something as lengthy as a novel it's not easy to keep all of the details straight as you're writing. Many times continuity problems will only show up in hindsight, during the revision process.

In real life, people act and react is a mostly predictable way based on their personalities and you should make sure your characters do as well. Establish your main character's personality very early on in your story and make sure their behavior is logical and consistent throughout the rest of the story. This allows your readers to feel like they're getting to know your character as they read scene after scene.

In addition to the personality quirks and traits of your characters, pay close attention to details like the style of their clothes, nicknames, possessions, appearance, and/or grooming habits. All of these aspects of your character must be believable and consistent throughout your story based the kind character you've created. When all of these things are in alignment, you will have created a believable character that comes alive in your story. If a certain character seems flat, give them a unique quirk or hobby and this will open up new avenues of thought that will make them seem more real.

No two characters are more important to flesh out in your story than your protagonist and antagonist. The objectives/goals of the protagonist and antagonist should be polar opposites. They should perform a complicated dance as they try to achieve their perspective goals while preventing the other from successfully achieving theirs. If done properly, this interplay between good and evil will leave readers captivated. This relationship between good and evil is the root of all good fiction. Both the hero and the villain must be equally interesting and complex. Most of us have seen the original Star Wars series of films and know the story well. George Lucas nails the perfect protagonist and antagonist relationship with Luke Skywalker and Darth Vader.

Ideally, you must get your reader to fear or hate your antagonist. But you also want your reader to identify with the antagonist emotionally in some way, without totally losing that loathing feeling. The antagonist in my first novel, Johann Pfizer is a textbook narcissist and sociopath but I am careful to also show some events in his life that helped to mold him into the monster he is. This creates a sort of sympathy in the reader. Johann displays violent behavior in several scenes of the novel and only hint to much greater sadistic tendencies. I've had many readers tell me this innuendo created suspense and made Johann seem even more sinister to them. Holding back or alluding to details of a character in the right way can make a reader's imagination run wild and form their own conclusions. Doing this connects the reader to your story on a much deeper level.

The reader should identify with your protagonist so strongly that they can't help but root for them against all odds. You must make your protagonist likeable or even lovable. A classic way to accomplish this connection between the reader and your protagonist is with sympathy. The protagonist in my first novel, Adam, is a stutterer with very low self-esteem but is incredibly intelligent. Adam's faced with nothing less than saving the world but has to overcome many of his personal obstacles before he can accomplish his supreme goal in the novel. Readers have told me that they root for Adam right away and connect with him because they draw a correlation between his struggles and their own. Getting readers to empathize with and relate to your character's struggles is another way emotional connections are created between them and your character.

One of my favorite questions to ask when doing a book club or other appearance before a small group is what is your favorite character in my novel and why? The answers I receive to this question provide valuable insight as to what attributes endear certain characters to the various types of readers. It's a truly rewarding experience when readers start referring to characters you've created as though they're real people. When this happens, you know you've done your job well.

The level of clarity in which you are able tell your story can either make or break you. Albert Einstein said, "If you can't explain it simply, you don't understand it well enough." Cut out the fluff and simply let your story do the talking. No matter how complex the story, you must make sure it can be easily understood by your reader. You achieve clarity by telling your story in the simplest language you can. When working on the first draft, if you feel the need to try to impress your reader with a vast vocabulary of overly complicated words then chances are the concept of your story needs more work.

Normally by the time an author reaches the end of the first draft of their first novel the quality of their writing becomes noticeably better. Insights about your plot, characters, and the story generally deepen. For this reason, the first couple of chapters of your story should be thoroughly re-examined after the first draft is completed. Often these first few chapters have to be heavily re-written so they mesh with the rest of your story. It may seem sacrilege, but it's even appropriate to consider whether or not one or both of the first two chapters can be eliminated altogether. Is your story leaner and more effective without these first few chapters? If so, they should go.

When revising, it is imperative that you make peace with the fact that anything in your story is expendable if it doesn't contribute to your story as a whole. Even if it's one of your favorite scenes, if it doesn't work the scene must be cut out or revised so there's more relevance. This was one of the most difficult things for me to become accustomed to. Becoming too emotionally invested in scenes that don't work for the greater good of your story is a huge impediment to crafting fiction that you're proud of. To create a cohesive story, you must make sure every scene connects with and resonates deeply with the scenes before and after it.

A common plot related issue to look for while revising is pacing problems. Pacing problems can sometimes be difficult for an author to see in their own work and for this reason many may be found by beta readers or even by a professional editor. Pacing issues are usually slow spots in your scenes where the action drags or, less often, scenes that are all action and no substance. The best cure for "slow scene syndrome" is to eliminate unnecessarily long sentences, tighten up excessive wordy descriptions, and liven up boring dialog.

Another culprit of slow scenes is too much narration at once. Page after page of narration is a sure way to bore your reader. The proper mix of narration and dialogue will keep things interesting and the plot moving forward. A great test of whether a scene needs to be cut or altered is to make a list of three reasons why that scene exists. If you can't come up with three good reasons it exists, it simply must go.

You will find some scenes in your story that move too quickly and end feeling like they might need more substance. You must find a way to infuse more depth into these scenes. This is accomplished best by showing rather than telling. Use your character's attitude, facial expressions and body language to convey things like their personality, fears, and motivations. You can also add details of the setting and the character to slow the scene down, add depth, and engage the reader.

The revision process can be hard and humbling work for a writer. Taking a scalpel to your beloved story is one of the most difficult things you will do. Chances are the excitement you originally felt when writing the first draft begins to fade, you are questioning your ability, and the whole process starts to feel like a chore. If you're anything like me, you will eventually get to the point where your spirit is almost broken and you feel like your entire story is crap. When this happens, it's important to step away and just simply take a break. Do a strenuous workout, mow the lawn, take the dog for a walk or whatever it takes to get you out of this negative frame of mind. Begin again when you're in a more positive mood and everything will seem better.

Beta Readers

Beta readers are like angels in the complicated

process of writing a good piece of fiction. They are often hardcore readers and even sometimes writers themselves. Once your story is polished by the revision process, the next step is to enlist the help of a few subjective pairs of eyes. Again, the role of a beta reader is to ferret out plot holes, problems with continuity, characterization or believability and they often do so free of charge. Chances are they'll find the last few stubborn typos hidden in your story as well. For my first novel, I created a Facebook group to recruit beta readers but there are also other options like writer's groups and online resources like Figment.com and Goodreads.com.

If using Facebook or any other social media to find beta readers, ask three or four times more people than you think you'll need, this will allow you to be choosy. It's likely that only a small percentage of the people you ask will have the time to read a novel and provide proper feedback. If you get more responses than you need, you can politely decline those readers who you feel won't be ideal for your project. When you send your invite be sure to include as many details as you can including a reasonable deadline for them, novel length, genre, and exactly what you're look for in terms of their feedback. If your prospective beta readers are also writers, offer to exchange manuscripts. People tend to give better feedback if they feel they're getting something in return.

When choosing a deadline, be sure to give the readers long enough to read the story and provide detailed feedback but it's important not to give them too long of a timeframe. Four to six weeks is adequate time for an average size novel, anything longer may encourage procrastination. Be straightforward and tell them you're only looking for honest feedback, not encouraging words. When the responses start rolling in, be choosey. You'll want to pick three to five readers for your final cut who you trust will be very honest and subjective.

All of the different perspectives you receive in their feedback will teach you a lot about your writing. Once you've received feedback from your beta readers and had time to digest it all, it's important to decide what feedback to use. Cast your ego aside and be as objective as possible when considering what to use and what not to use. A successful writing career will humble you more than almost anything else I can think of. Try to remember that creating a cohesive and compelling story is your ultimate goal. After the editing, revising and beta reader steps have been completed now your manuscript ready for a professional editor!

Choosing an Editor

Choosing the right editor for your book is essential to the quality of your book and your reputation as an author. Very few authors have the objectivity to create a book that's ready for the market without an extra set of very well trained eyes. It's not enough to find an editor that is good, but they must be the right fit for you and your project. The Editorial Freelancer's Association's website (http://www.the-efa.org) is one place to begin your search. You can also call any local schools in your area that teach writing to adults to inquire about editor referrals.

If your budget is small then you might have to choose an editor with fewer credentials and less experience. Don't be overly concerned that you'll get what you paid for in this regard, less experience doesn't mean that an editor isn't great at what they do. An editor who is charging less than their competition might be just starting out and trying to build their client base and reputation. Some editors charge by the hour, others charge by the word. For a 300 page novel you can expect to pay anywhere from $300 to $1,200 depending upon the editor's reputation and experience.

Before you make a commitment to an editor,

request a few references of past clients and contact one or two to gauge their feedback. It's also wise to ask the editor to work through a chapter of your manuscript together before you sign a contract. After working together for one chapter, you should have an idea of whether or not the editor is the right fit for your work. Any reputable editor should be willing to do these two things, if not, be cautious. If you don't think a particular editor is right for your story, keep looking. There's no shortage of competent editors to choose from.

PART III

Marketing Your Book

Chapter Fifteen

Applying Lessons Learned in the Business World

Those of us who have had to work a full time job while launching a writing career know that it's no easy task, for a variety of reasons. What people sometimes fail to realize is working a day job that has nothing to do with writing can also give you a huge advantage. Being in the workforce can teach you many valuable lessons that can be applied directly to your writing career.

Building Your Brand

Look at any successful writer's career and all of them have effectively coined their "brand." This is your own unique voice or way of telling a story, once developed it's a golden thread that runs through all of your projects and will keep core readers who resonate with your style coming back for more. Pay close attention to what all of your writing has in common in terms of genre and voice and continue to move in this direction. Working in your intended genre should feel natural and organic, like breathing. When you have identified your natural "brand" this will be the key to attracting your niche readership.

Be Punctual

Respect other people's time, this one simple act will gain you a lot of respect in any business, especially creative careers. Let's face it; creative people (myself included) can be scatterbrained and lackadaisical. There is an incredibly talented pool of writers out there and the competition is fierce. Make a serious effort to set yourself apart from the crowd by becoming trustworthy and a pleasure to do business with.

Deliver on Your Promises

You must prove to the world that you're serious about your career. I learned a valuable secret from working in my corporate career, habitually under promise and over deliver. This not only has a tendency to impress but it takes pressure off you when trying to juggle many responsibilities at once. If you think you can complete a project in a month, promise it in a month and a half or two months. You will quickly establish a reputation with everyone you deal with for being the rock star that you are.

Practice Respect

Be respectful and professional with everyone and try to "Pay It Forward" when you can. Whether people are several rungs higher on the ladder than you are or just on the ground floor of the business, they all deserve the same amount of respect. Along with the quality of your work, your reputation is your greatest asset. Once you've achieved a certain amount of success in your career, writers will flock to you for advice. At times it can feel overwhelming.

It has become my practice, as often as possible, to share what I have learned and offer advice when asked. This is one of the main reasons I wanted to write this book. I feel a great affinity towards anyone undertaking creative endeavors, especially writing, it's a hard road but sharing the lessons you have learned can save another writer from the pain of your mistakes and help to provide them with the quantum leap they need to be successful.

Stay Positive

Keep your communications positive when posting on your social media outlets. With time, it is very easy to get comfortable and start posting details of your personal life. This is okay to do sometimes because people are naturally curious but it is best to keep the more negative aspects of your life off social media and to keep certain aspects of your personal life, well, personal. Attract the quality of readers you want by keeping your communications positive. Lift people up, don't bring them down and they will reward you for it by coming back.

Also, you will find some readers who "like" your author page may also search your personal social media accounts and request you as a personal friend. Although I value my readers greatly, for obvious reasons, I'm very selective about who I let into my personal life. If I have no personal connection with a person, I do not accept the invitation to connect to my personal account. As your writing career progresses, this practice becomes increasingly important.

Utilize All Available Resources

Take advantage of any in-house courses that

you can apply to your writing career or tuition reimbursement that the company you work for provides. Once you begin to view your day job not as a curse or a burden but as a stepping stone and opportunity to further enhance your writing career, it can really spark a shift in perception that improves your mood and outlook as well as the quality of your day to day life.

Chapter Sixteen

Studying Success

We can shorten our own path to achieving the writer's life by studying the different ways other authors have found success. Their stories can provide us with more than proven ideas, they can also provide us with much needed inspiration to persevere and keep striving for our next goal. The fact that other authors are taking charge of their futures by dreaming up new and different ways to propel their careers into the stratosphere is proof that, with ingenuity and today's technology, anything is possible. The only limit is our imaginations.

Veronica Roth, author of the wildly successful Divergent trilogy of novels, wrote her first novel at the age of twenty-one during her senior year at Northwestern University in Chicago. She admits that she completed the first draft of the book in forty days while studying for finals. This was inspiring to me, if she could create something so successful in forty days while completing her finals then I can no longer make excuses about working a day job and not having the time to write anything of length. Veronica attended writer's conferences during her junior year at college to network with others in the business of writing and to secure a literary agent. It was apparent that she was actively learning about the business well before her novel was even completed.

In the first book, Veronica weaves a dystopian tale of a Chicago, one hundred years in the future, where society is separated into five predetermined factions: Abnegation (The Selfless); Erudite (The Intelligent); Dauntless (The Brave); Amity (The Peaceful); and Candor (The Honest). Before the sequel to Divergent was released, her publisher launched a quiz on social media so readers could, "discover their faction." This was a great marketing idea that endears readers to Veronica Roth's trilogy of books by allowing them to envision their place inside her futuristic dystopian world.

Using his already extensive social media platform author John Green managed to get his most recent book, "The Fault in Our Stars" on the New York Times best-seller list before it was even published! He did this by promising to autograph each pre-ordered copy.

John and his brother, singer Hank Green, began building their massive fan base in 2006 with the Brotherhood 2.0. project on YouTube which initially was a poorly watched challenge between the two brothers to create a video for each other every weekday instead of communicating via text messages. At the time John had already published two books, one had received a major literary award and the second book achieved mild success, but neither books were bestsellers. The brothers have continued producing and posting videos to YouTube and now have millions of followers.

John Green also encourages his fans called, "Nerdfighters" (or collectively as Nerdfighteria) to leave handwritten notes between the pages of his books in libraries and bookstores as well as other places Nerdfighters frequent for other Nerdfighters to find. This has become a phenomena that has taken on a life all of its own.

The author of the Fifty Shades of Grey series, E.L. James built readership using an incremental approach. James built and impressive fan base on FanFiction.net where she published a series of her stories based on the Twilight series. After her readership base was formed, she changed the names of the characters and then self-published the stories in book form releasing it on her own website. She then used a series of writer's blogs to promote the series until it was picked up by a division of Random House publishing in 2012. The series is now a household name.

There are countless other stories similar to these. Harness the awesome power of the internet and invest the time in searching for other stories, it will be time well spent. Reading about how other authors have become successful will make you think in entirely new and different ways. I guarantee it will spark original ideas of your own. This is how the brain of a creative works, from one idea is born another.

To find success as an Indie author we must find a way to build an audience of readers willing to buy our books. To increase your odds it is a good idea to begin building this readership base as early as possible, ideally before you publish your first book.

I did just the opposite, focusing on building a following after publishing my first novel. Luckily,

I have found success anyways.

Just as importantly, you must find a way to transform readers into fans who do more than buy and read your books. A true fan is someone who feels they have a personal interest in you and your success, someone who identifies or actually weaves aspects and ideas of your stories into their life. By doing so you build an extremely loyal group of readers who frequently extol your book's virtues to others. If you manage to accomplish this, you will almost be assured success of your book as well as future projects.

Chapter Seventeen

Adopting the Collaborative Mentality

Marketing is just another term for sharing your work in a deliberate way with the goal of gaining a fan base and generating sales. The phrase, "It Takes A Village..." very much applies to starting a writing career from scratch. My marketing knowledge took a quantum leap from a single forty-five minute call with the very successful author and motivational speaker, Grace Daly. What Grace taught me was as invaluable as it was Zen-like.

As Indie authors with small budgets we must take the time to think about who our natural collaborators are. Often they are companies or individuals who offer a product or service that mesh with your book in some way, the larger the organization the better. These large companies already have a huge promotional outreach and great marketing expertise. Collaborations such as this can help you reach a much larger audience than you could on your own.

For instance, I wore a pair of Moscot Lemtosh glasses in some of my promotional headshots for my first novel. I purchased these eyeglass frames only because I liked them but shortly after my call with Grace, I decided to reach out to the Moscot company to see if there was an opportunity to collaborate. They informed me that there was a segment on their Facebook called, "Eye Spy" where they post pictures of people wearing their frames. Not only did they agree to post my headshot but they also included a link to my novel. This got me lots of international publicity as well as many new followers from all over the world on my Facebook author page, and it didn't cost me a penny.

This same strategy is appropriate with your own works as well. Think of promotional campaigns in which you can bundle multiple projects of your own together and offer them as a package deals and market your work in different ways that generate multiple revenue streams. For example, I have published a few books of my poetry and got a favorable response. I decided to start offering individual autographed prints of poems that were published in those collections for sale online. This was incredibly easy to do and very little work because I print them only as they're ordered. To be successful as an Indie writer it's important to apply the same creativity that makes you a great writer to the marketing side of your business. Go crazy with your ideas! Outside of the box thinking will garner great rewards.

Grassroots, local marketing is very useful as

well. Look for ways to get your book into the hands of the people in your own community. In the city I live in, they have a program called, "Little Libraries." These are small weatherproof bookcases that people can install in their front yards and people can borrow or donate any books they wish. I've donated several copies of my books to these Little Libraries.

Another great way to branch out is to write freelance articles for publications that are in alignment with the subject matter of your writing. Many online publications will allow you to post a short biography and a few links of your choosing along with your articles. The two links I always post are to my blog and my Facebook author page. Even if you don't get paid to write these pieces, the exposure can be invaluable.

Once you change your way of thinking to the collaborative mentality, you begin to discover countless untapped opportunities that were there all along. Even if you self-publish, remember, you don't have to do it alone. Your odds of success in the publishing business are much greater if you have an army of allies willing to assist you along the way. I've discovered that people actually want to help. It's only a matter of finding a business relationship that makes sense for all parties involved.

Chapter Eighteen

Ways to Build Your Audience Online

Authors today are so lucky to have social media as an opportunity to connect with vast amounts of readers online. So many authors underutilize this valuable resource to build readership because to do so effectively is tricky and many times counterintuitive. It took me years to learn how to effectively build a following online for my writing and in this chapter I want to share with you the most important lessons I've learned.

Create a blog and post to it regularly. In the last few years, Facebook and Twitter have stolen a lot of the limelight, but never underestimate the value of a good old-fashioned blog. Contributing regularly to a blog (a la Wordpress or Tumblr) serves the dual purpose of keeping your writing skills razor sharp while attracting precious readers and learning what keeps them engaged. People who follow blogs tend to be the kind of reader that is willing delve a little deeper and spend more than just a few seconds reading your work. Be sure to create a page on your blog including links to your other social media accounts as well as any websites where you or your writing is featured. Make it easy for people to find your online presence.

Marketing is hard work, it also takes you away from writing, so think of ways to make the best use of your time and work smarter. Link up your Facebook, Twitter, Blog, and any other social media accounts in such a way that when you post something to one it will automatically post to the others. This also creates consistent content across all of your social media platforms and is a more efficient by freeing up more of your time to do what you love, write. Don't forget to create a LinkedIn account to promote your writing. LinkedIn is growing fast and should not be overlooked. The online world moves fast so try to keep abreast of new social media sites. If you see a new social media site whose demographic is in alignment with your target readership, by all means open an account and start using it to your advantage.

One major thing I've learned about building an audience online is that the right kind of generosity is rewarded. I run a several promotions on my Facebook author page. One of which is called, "Reader Appreciation Friday" where I have book giveaways. I offer a free five-chapter sample of my novel to the first person who responds with their email address. This sample is long enough for people to get immersed into the story and then I added links at the end where they can purchase the full version of the book. I found this to be a great way to connect with readers and build an email list for future marketing. The wrong kind of giving can backfire. Originally, I was giving away the full version of the eBook on Reader Appreciation Friday but people stopped buying my books because they were waiting to win the promotion, which they knew would come every Friday!

I also run another regular Facebook promotion that has proven to be very popular called, "Showcase Saturday." On Saturdays, I allow other writers to post their writing with links and readers to post works of their favorite authors on my Facebook page. This works for me because many of my readers are also authors. I know how difficult this profession is and I am thrilled to now be in a position to be able to make a difference in helping other authors get their work recognized. It also gives me a day off promoting on Facebook, which can be hard work.

EBooks typically cost you nothing to give away so don't be afraid to give the full version of your book away occasionally. Promotions like that are fun and will help you create a buzz about your projects. I will even occasionally give away physical copies of my novel. Whenever I travel I make it a point to bring a couple autographed copies of my book and will give them away randomly to strangers I cross paths with. I'm making others happy and view the cost as an investment in the future of my writing career.

I began offering a book club discount on social media for book club orders of five or more copies. As an added bonus, I also include a complimentary thirty-minute FaceTime/Skype video call with book clubs who took advantage of the deal to join them in their discussion of the book. This has been a great way to create a buzz about my books as well as a way to further connect with readers all over the world.

Pay close attention to which promotions work and which don't, then shift your time and energy towards what gets results. When promoting on social media especially, make note of what engages readers and whatever works, do more of it. Keep trying new things until you find promotions that translate into page likes and book sales.

I've found that boosting posts on Facebook (paying Facebook to place your posts in the news feeds of strangers) might increase your total outreach but doesn't always translate into as many page likes or book purchases as you might think. Facebook will allow you to choose age/gender as well as include interests for people you're targeting for your promotion. For example, I typically choose an age range of 18 to 55 and include keywords such as "Fiction, Literature, Reading, etc." The more targeted the promotion, the better results you will see. At the time of the writing of this book Facebook doesn't allow you to target your promotions this way from a smartphone, you must be on a computer.

By all means, if you don't have one already, purchase and learn how to utilize a smartphone. My phone allows me to access my blog, website and all of my social media sites on the go with my smartphone. The smartphone has become an indispensable tool in my writing career because it makes me so much more productive as a writer. When traveling, we all typically have multiple hours where we are just waiting, so why not use this time to be productive? I can now use this time to create new pieces or work on marketing by posting new promotional content to social media.

I hope you find these tips on building your online audience to be helpful. To be a successful indie author you must learn how to be as efficient as you can. It's imperative to get the largest outreach you can, in the shortest amount of time for the least amount of money. If you work hard, work smart, and are patient, you'll have the online readership that you've always wished for.

Chapter Nineteen

Ways to Build Your Audience Offline

Building readership is of the utmost importance for all authors who wish to make a living and a name for themselves. You must have readers to sell books to. Finding readers who connect with your work is never as easy as you think it will be. Following are some tips for earning readers that I've learned in my twenty years of writing.

There's no shame in talking about yourself and your writing. When someone asks what you do tell proudly them you're an author, even if you're still working a day job to help pay the bills! This will almost always open up a conversation in which you can tell them what you're currently working on. Even if you're an introvert you'll get better at this each time you try it. One on one conversations are a wonderful way to build readership at a grassroots level. Remember, at any time you could be crossing paths with someone who either has the power to help your career in a big way or knows someone who can. Building a successful writing career relies on effectively selling yourself.

Be genuine, always. If you stick to this adage, you will be creating your own individual brand with each interaction and every word you write. Each of us are unique, gifted with our own voice and perspective. Don't try to be anyone but yourself when conducting business face-to-face as well as in your writing. People will sense your honesty, respect you for it and you will more likely find the audience that's already out there searching for you.

Have business cards on you at all times, especially when traveling. In terms of business card design, think simple and classic. In this digital age it might seem old fashioned but business cards will always be an effective tool. When you start to chat it up with that stranger sitting next to you on the plane, a business card will allow you to leave them with something to remember you by. I've had many book sales from people who I've met in airports or on planes.

To be a successful author you must continuously study the market of the genre you specialize in. Brainstorm about ways to cross-sell your books. Which organizations or businesses would have a customer base that would seem like a natural fit for what you write? For example, I had the opportunity to help teach a corporate meditation seminar for an insurance company. At the end of the seminar, naturally, I mentioned my book on meditation and where it could be purchased. I also chatted with audience members afterwards and told them about some of my other book titles. This resulted in sales of three of my titles.

Always have your eyes open and be actively learning about how other successful authors are promoting their books. Don't spend time following those who are at your level, carefully study the marketing techniques of those authors who are already where you want to be on the ladder of success. Discover what works for these authors in regard to attracting readers and try the techniques for yourself. Be careful to use your own style and voice in your marketing efforts.

Seek out neighborhood and hometown newspapers and tell them you are a local author who would like to promote a specific project and ask about interview opportunities. Most newspapers have room in their publications for local interest stories and are very willing to work with you. My very first published piece was a poem that appeared in a neighborhood newspaper when I was in my early twenties. This appearance in the neighborhood newspaper opened the door to opportunities for articles in my hometown newspaper, "The Columbus Dispatch". In the writing business, you will quickly learn that one opportunity truly does lead into another.

There's nothing that polishes your communication style and your writing like getting up in front of a live audience to read your work. Scour your local media for open mic nights at bookstores, coffee houses, or pubs that will give you a chance to read your work in front of a live audience and build a readership base. Audience reaction is an instant barometer of what works and what doesn't and will teach you a whole lot in a small amount of time. People develop a deep admiration for authors who are confident enough to do this. Plan on having books on hand for sale at these events even if you have leave them in your car. If the establishment allows you to mention this during your reading, great but if not you can mention it while mingling with the audience after your reading.

Offer discounts on your self-published books to book clubs. I personally offer 15% off orders of five books or more to book clubs. You can also make yourself available to appear at local book club meetings that are featuring your book to have an open discussion about your career and work, answer questions, and autograph copies. Book club appearances are one of my favorite things to do because they offer you the rare opportunity to connect with your reader in a more intimate setting. If you make a good impression with a book club you can almost guarantee both word of mouth advertising and future customers of your next book.

For those out of book clubs appearances that are too far away to travel to I also offer a complimentary virtual book club appearance via

FaceTime or Skype with a thirty-minute question and answer session. Although this can never be as personal as a face-to-face appearance, this is a fun and easy way to expand your readership base worldwide.

Contact managers of independent bookstores, coffee houses, or pubs and ask if they ever host author events. These can be poetry/book readings or book signing events. I've had better luck with businesses that are located near college campuses. Coffee houses and pub readings are often times as easy as getting on their list and showing up whenever the event is scheduled. Bookstores can be trickier; they want to make sure you can draw a crowd. In my experience, bookstore managers aren't always willing to agree to hosting an appearance or signing event right away. But once your book is on their shelves for a while and you've proven that people are willing to purchase it, they are much more open hosting an event for you.

Contact station managers at local public or college radio stations and explain that you're a local author and you'd be interested in doing a radio interview about your most recent project. As a rule, people who listen to public radio are typically readers and are more willing to give local unknown authors a chance. However small the audience, with each media interview you take part in you will gain skills and become more engaging, comfortable, and relaxed. The whole secret to a successful media interview is to just be yourself.

Search for writing or poetry contests in your area. The city of Saint Paul, where I live offers an annual contest called, "Sidewalk Poetry" in which they imprint the poems of winning local poets in freshly poured neighborhood sidewalks throughout the city. The winning poets also have the opportunity to read their work and appear on the local news. Most of these contests do require an entry fee but this is usually a nominal amount and they typically help to support the local arts community.

Consider volunteering your time for community organizations and charities that are tied to the arts. This will allow you to meet other creative people in your community with similar interests and you may cross paths with someone who can teach you something useful or even a true mentor who can teach you on deeper levels. Magical things can happen when creative folks get together it can help to spark ideas that you never would think of on your own.

Marketing yourself offline is a powerful way to build your writing career and should not be overlooked. Sure, you can reach many more people by marketing online but face to face interactions can make much more impact and spark word of mouth advertising that's so crucial to build an author fan base.

You should never stop thinking of effective

marketing ideas for your work. In fact, I make it a point to jot down at least three new marketing ideas per week. Not all of these will be winners but some of them are. Sometimes one idea leads to another. Once you train your brain to generate these new ideas on a consistent basis you'll be surprised at how easy and natural this process becomes. Ideas cost nothing and they are truly endless, you need to use every advantage you can find to make it in this business. Start making your ideas work for you.

Chapter Twenty

The Potential Role of Literary Journals

Early in my writing career, I encountered the same conundrum time and time again. Major publishers wanted prospective authors who were represented by a literary agent and most literary agents wouldn't accept unpublished authors. I'm almost embarrassed to admit it but it took almost twenty years of struggling as an Indie author for me to discover one important piece of the literary puzzle that I was missing in my career, submitting my poetry and short stories to literary journals. Throughout those two decades I was reading everything I could find in terms of writing craft and tips on getting published and don't recall seeing literary journals submissions mentioned even once.

It took advice from a very well educated friend who also writes poetry to clue me in on the vital piece that I was missing to help build my writing career She explained how being published in literary journals can greatly increase your odds of being accepted by a literary agent and/or publisher and how these publishing credentials are an indispensable addition to your writing resume. Although this may be common knowledge in the world of academia it's not so widely known in the Indie author circles.

This aforementioned friend was also kind enough to submit a packet of five of my poems to a few journals and I was pleasantly surprised by the results. I was accepted by three literary journals. What happened next was even far more fabulous. When the editor of one of the literary journals learned that I was working on this book on writing she offered to publish, in addition to my poems, a short story and a book review to help promote the book! I was ecstatic. It was a triple play, further proof of what I always found to be true about the writing profession, one job usually always leads to other opportunities.

The literary journal submission process is easy and isn't very time consuming for most literary journals. In regard to finding literary journals open to submission, remember, Google is your friend. If you have access to a computer and the internet or a smartphone you have a world of knowledge at your fingertips. Poets and Writer's Magazine offers a very comprehensive list of literary journals on their website (http://www.pw.org/literary_magazines). The Council of Literary Magazines and Presses' website (http://www.clmp.org/about/dir.html) offers a lot of useful information as well.

You can also find an abundance of useful

information by searching the internet yourself. Learn to think in search terms such as, "Literary Magazines for New Poets", "Submitting Poetry or Short Stories to Literary Journals" or using similar search phrases. Search engines will quickly help you find what you're looking for. When you discover a few journals that match your style or genre of writing just look for their submission guidelines on their websites. Many websites will have a submission guideline link prominently displayed on their homepage.

Literary journals fall in different categories based on size and level of respect in the literary world. The larger and more prestigious the journal, obviously, the more difficult it will be to get your work published in as a new author. There are mid-range journals which are a little easier and finally the smaller journals that you are the most likely to get your work published in. During my first round of submissions, I asked my friend to submit to a variety of all three tiers of journals.

Some journals offer payment, most do not but any details about payment should be found in the publication's submission information.

Many literary journals now accept online submissions, which allows you to submit to a larger number of journals in a shorter amount of time. A cover letter is a requirement for most journals and my advice is to keep this very simple. One or two lines are generally all that is necessary and remember to include a short biography. Response times usually vary. They can be as fast as a day and as a slow as a year and a half.

Before you begin submitting, it's wise to create an email account that you use just for submissions. This way you won't accidentally miss any responses that get buried in your personal email account. Once you begin the submission process it's a good idea to create an email folder labeled, "Literary Journal Submissions" and file all of your submission emails away there. Likewise, create an email folder for editor's acceptances of your work.

Once you find out how easy it is to submit to literary journals you will likely be doing this frequently so it's also important to track your submissions. If you don't keep track of what work was submitted, and to which publications, it can become a big long-term problem. Tracking your submissions isn't a lot of work, just create a spreadsheet with a few columns, listing when your work was sent out and then updating it to reflect acceptance or rejection. Otherwise, the same piece might be rejected by the same journal twice, or you may lose track of when your work will be published.

Many times the publication dates for the journals who accept your work can be anywhere from a few months to a year in the future. Be sure to keep track of the dates your work will appear in these journals and when the day comes post a link to your published work on all of your social media accounts and enthusiastically announce it to your readers. I will typically set a reminder on my iPhone to alert me a few days before my work is published to remind me to post links to my social media accounts.

Keep a spreadsheet of where you were published, the date your work appeared, and the piece that was published. This is an important part of your writer's resume. Lastly, don't forget to celebrate because each time you get published it is a victory that will get you that much closer to living your ideal writer's life!

Additional Resources

I hope this book helps you on your amazingly difficult, wonderfully frustrating, and unbelievably rewarding journey that I call the writer's life. If you continue to learn, evolve, clearly define your goals, and network with other creative people you will eventually attain whatever level of success it is you seek. No matter where you are in your writing career at the present moment, you should be very proud of who you are and what you do. No matter how difficult it might feel, never give up. If you are a real writer, you have to write, you have no say in the matter. We are all part of the brotherhood and sisterhood of the pen and our lineage stretches back millennia. We are the entertainers and the teachers, the keepers of the past and the shapers of the future.

It's my firm belief that if we keep an open heart

and mind, continue learning and practicing our craft the writing only gets better with age and practice. This profession we share, this love of words, can be pure magic and the impact of the work you do has the potential to stretch well beyond the day your last word is written. Write well and may your journey continue for a very long time.

Here are a few additional resources to help you on your way.

Books

The Elements of Style - William Strunk Jr., E.B. White, and Roger Angell

This book is essential to any writer's library and is filled with practical advice on craft. Check it out from the library, in a few minutes you'll realize what a treasure it is and then you'll have to purchase a copy.

Writer's Market - Robert Lee Brewer

Writer's Market is re-released every year with updated information. This is the book to buy if you're planning on submitting your work to publishers of any genre.

Bird by Bird: Some Instruction on Writing and Life - Anne Lamott

This is not a book on how to write. Bird by Bird is a very philosophical and reflective book that will remind you why it is you love to write. After reading this, you'll come away with a much deeper appreciation for your craft and creativity in general.

Choose Yourself - James Altucher

Choose Yourself provides valuable insight as well as inspiration on how to shift to the entrepreneurial mode of thinking that's so essential to becoming a successful indie writer. This book will also convince you that in our unstable job market the absolute worst thing you can do is stop pursuing your passion for the "security" of working for someone else.

Daily Rituals: How Artists Work - Mason Currey

Daily Rituals makes us creative folks realize we're not alone in our strangeness, there are really others like us! The book gives concrete examples of how other creatives have learned to harness the awesome power of their creativity. This book forces you to think about crafting a daily ritual of your own that makes the most of your talents.

Online Resources

Owl Writing Lab - https://owl.english.purdue.edu

This site offers hundreds of free resources that help you become a better writer.

Writer's Digest - http://www.writersdigest.com

This website offers useful information for almost every aspect of writing from education to getting published. There are also forums you can join to connect with other writers.

The Elements of Style - http://www.bartleby.com/141/index.html

A basic, online version of the book recommended above. Originally published in 1918, this still is an indispensable resource for writers.

Poets and Writers - http://www.pw.org

A good resource for writing in general. I've found this site especially helpful for the "Grants and Awards" and "Conferences and Residencies" pages. Contests are a wonderful way to build your writing resume and offer the chance of making a little extra income as well.

About Eric Vance Walton

Eric Vance Walton is a novelist, author, and poet with a writing career spanning nearly two decades. He has self-published several books in genres, including his debut novel Alarm Clock Dawn. Eric's poetry has appeared in literary journals such as Page and Spine, The Stray Branch, and Leaves of Ink. He invites you to visit his Facebook page, "Eric Vance Walton, Author".

About Authors Publish Press

Authors Publish Press is dedicated to supporting the careers of writers. We publish books, eBooks, and an e-magazine.

To learn more about us, visit AuthorsPublish.com/Press/

We encourage you to sign up for our free magazine at AuthorsPublish.com. We send you publishers accepting submissions of creative writing.

CPSIA information can be obtained at www.ICGtesting.com
Printed in the USA
LVOW12s2149180615

443065LV00001B/2/P

9 781942 344001